Endorsements for Learning to Fly...

'The first generation of knowledge management has come and gone. The second generation, which promises both deeper insights and greater impact, will be less about data and more about the social nature of knowledge, less about "capture and retrieval" and more about innovating and sharing, and ultimately more about know-how rather than know about – the only knowledge that ultimately matters in any pragmatic institution.

BP's dramatic ascent as an industry leader stems in no small part from its commitment to learning and knowledge. Chris Collison and Geoff Parcell show how new ideas and tools are making working and learning inseparable in one of the world's most innovative large companies.'

Peter Senge, Senior Lecturer, MIT, and
Chair, SOL (Society for Organizational Learning)

'Collison and Parcell compellingly demonstrate how the combination of sharing behaviors, smart processes and enabling technology have made BP a world leader in knowledge management.'

Steve Ballmer, President and Chief Executive Officer,
Microsoft Corporation

'There are very few knowledge management books written by actual practitioners and this is one of them. BP has led the charge in KM and these authors were there. A fine place to start one's KM education!'

Larry Prusak, Executive Director,
IBM Institute for Knowledge Management

'In the last five years few companies have implemented their knowledge management strategy as effectively as BP. Chris Collison and Geoff Parcell have used this compelling experience to provide a thoughtful and action-oriented guide to knowledge management. It should be required reading for both students, practitioners and, perhaps most important, for those executives that have to deliver on the promise of leveraging knowledge assets as a mechanism for gaining competitive advantage.

Dr John C. Henderson, Richard C. Shipley Professor of Management,
Boston University

'A great story of a global company on the journey toward the Knowledge Driven World. From building networks across the organization to "having the time to halve the time" it is a journey of constant change for the better.'

Robert H. Buckman, Chairman and CEO, Buckman ~

D09976372

'With distinctive clarity and simplicity, Learning to Fly combines real practice with rich experience to meet the need to leverage know-how in a network-centric world. The authors have codified a set of proven tools and processes for teams and organisations to learn before, during and after, in order to dramatically improve their performance.'

Kent Greenes, Chief Knowledge Officer, SAIC

'Finally in the jungle of theoretical sources about knowledge management, a really practical, "hands-on" book which gives useful insights in the practice: How to initiate knowledge management and even more important how to keep it alive – as normal part of everyday business.'

Cordula Söfftge, BMW Group Learning Concepts

'There are plenty of theoretical books on knowledge management around, but Learning to Fly takes a uniquely practical approach. This compelling account brings the subject alive, because it is written by people who actually did the work in one of the world's largest companies.'

Mark Bennett,
Rio Tinto Knowledge Management Team, Perth, Western Australia

'This excellent book is a one-stop shop for all knowledge management practitioners who want to start, or enliven a KM initiative in their organiza- tions. Full of stories, lessons learned and sound advice, and yet based on strong theoretical grounds; the book is serious, educational and fun to read. As both academic and KM practitioner, I would recommend it for students and colleagues.'

Dr Ora Setter, Faculty of Management, Tel Aviv University

'As relevant and practical a guide to creating value through knowledge management as you could wish for.'

Laura Cochran, Head of Knowledge Management, CGNU plc

'There is no substitute for learning from experience, especially in a field as new as knowledge management. Chris Collison and Geoff Parcell have distilled the real nuggets from their years of practical implementation experi- ence at BP. This book's clear, readable format, filled with specific tips and helpful anecdotes, is a demonstration of the co-authors' skill in transferring knowledge. Read it and apply its lessons – you will save yourself months of effort.'

Elizabeth Lank, Programme Director, Mobilising Knowledge, ICL

'We've known BP as a learning organisation for some time, this book demonstrates powerfully that they are also a sharing organisation.'

Barbara Stocking, Regional Director, South East NHS Executive

'Collison and Parcell have generously shared their practical experiences and lessons learned in one of the leading global communities of knowledge-BP. Their journey to help and enable "knowers" to better share their knowledge and learn from each other highlights the key to achieving sustainable competitive advantage. In an easy-to-read style, the authors share much useful knowledge on methods and practices to overcome barriers and create the environment that people want and need to reach full potential. This is a book that is easy to recommend.'

George Birchfield, Vice President, Solomon Associates Inc.

'This book gives an enlightening, and practical approach to knowledge management with excellent examples of what can be achieved. It is essential reading for all levels of management who are likely to become involved in the knowledge management process.'

Paul Lester, Group Managing Director, Balfour Beatty

'Learning from BP's refreshingly practical approach to knowledge management is helping the Department of Trade and Industry to meet its aspiration to put itself at the forefront of Knowledge Management.'

Pat Langford, Assistant Director, Knowledge Management Unit, Department of Trade and Industry

'BP have come up with that rare thing – a process that is transferable across cultures and organisations. It's powerful yet simple, accommodates change yet is rooted in the commonality of human needs in facing challenges. It feels right that a process that aids learning from drilling an oil well should aid learning from responding to a natural disaster – because both endeavours have humans at their source. We copied and pasted the approach to Tearfund, and it's helping us to learn from our successes and failures to keep improving the way we do things. In this age of continuous change, it is a real asset to help the organisation to cope, to adapt and move forward.'

Paul Whiffen, Knowledge Manager, TEAR Fund

'Learning is when knowledge is applied to action and something changes. We know this is true, yet it is often difficult to put the theory into practice. Collison and Parcell describe how that transfer was achieved in BP and by articulating it so clearly, they make it possible for others to learn.'

Eve Mitleton-Kelly, Director of the Complexity & Organisational Learning Research Programme at the London School of Economics and Executive Coordinator of SOL-UK (London)

' "Learning Organisations" and "Knowledge Management" are words often used in the HR world but are they really understood? How do you capture and share the acquired experience and good practice held in the heads of hundreds or thousands of employees? Organisations that successfully answer this question can gain genuine competitive advantage. The approach and tools that described here are as applicable to the Telecoms industry as they are to BP and, I believe, are of value to any organisation endeavouring to unlock the secrets of knowledge management.'

Rob Meakin, Director of Human Resources, Marconi

'Here's what we have been waiting for – a practical way to apply Knowledge Management for immediate and identifiable business success. The authors have extensive experience in doing that and we should listen to them carefully. Just in time too, as the challenges of the future – wireless Internet, e-Business, continuing mergers, de-mergers and globalization – demand that we get on with the business of KM and this book makes that possible. Well done, guys.'

Colonel Ed Guthrie, US Army (retired)

Learning
to **Fly**

Practical Lessons from one of the World's Leading Knowledge Companies

Chris **Collison** & Geoff **Parcell**

CAPSTONE

Copyright © Chris Collison and Geoff Parcell 2001

The right of Chris Collison and Geoff Parcell to be identified as the authors of this work
has been asserted in accordance with the Copyright, Designs and Patents Act 1988

First published 2001 by
Capstone Publishing, Inc.   Capstone Publishing Limited
40 Commerce Park   8 Newtec Place
Milford   Oxford OX4 1RE
CT 06460   United Kingdom
USA   http://www.capstone.co.uk
Contact: info@capstonepub.com

CIP catalogue records for this book are available from the British Library
and the US Library of Congress

ISBN 1-84112-124-X

Typeset in 10.5/13 pt Plantin by
Sparks Computer Solutions Ltd, Oxford, UK
http://www.sparks.co.uk
Printed and bound by
TJ International Ltd, Padstow, Cornwall

This book is printed on acid-free paper

Substantial discounts on bulk quantities of Capstone books are available to
corporations, professional associations and other organizations. If you are in the
USA or Canada, phone the LPC Group, Special Sales Department for details on
(1-800-626-4330) or fax (1-800-334-3892). Everywhere else, phone Capstone
Publishing on (+44-1865-798623) or fax (+44-1865-240941).

This book is dedicated to:

Stella, Chris and Bronwyn

Louise, Martha and Hannah,
who came into this world between Chapters 11 and 12

CONTENTS

It is important to find a way of capturing what has been
learned, in order that it can be reused by others, sometimes
immediately and at other times after a distinct time lag.

You know when sharing knowledge has become an
unconscious competence, when there are no longer
people dedicated to knowledge management in the
organisation, when the techniques are embedded in the
core business processes.

Our intent was to write a book that was both practical
and pragmatic, to help people take their first steps to do
something different in order that they could learn from
that and adapt further. Did we achieve that, if not what
was the difference and why was it different? What can
we learn from that?

FOREWORD

No one can tell the story of what a company does, and its character better than the people who work for it.

Over the last few years BP has grown, organically and through mergers and combinations, and is now one of the largest companies in the oil and gas industry. Size alone, of course, means nothing. Size didn't save the dinosaur.

The potential value of size, which is there for us to capture, is the knowledge held by 100,000 of the world's brightest people. Knowledge of a particular technology, a relationship, a way of doing business, which has been proved successful. The value comes from sharing that knowledge and applying it in different places and different situations.

This collection of real-life stories describes a company that is just beginning to learn how to learn, and people who are just starting to share the knowledge.

People like Marton Haga, an engineer from Norway who realised he was using a combination of drilling tools in an unusual way, and achieving a dramatic improvement in performance by so doing. An improvement worth around $300,000. He put his ideas on the BP intranet, and the very next day they were read by his colleagues in Trinidad who were able to use them to achieve comparable gains.

People like Fumu Mondoloka, our marketing manager in Cape Town, who asked for help from a marketing network that stretches across the company, and who received by return ideas from the team in Aberdeen, which made possible a breakthrough in his thinking and made it possible for him to secure a significant new deal, selling lubricants in Tanzania.

I hope this book will inspire others to achieve similar sharing of knowledge – within BP and beyond. Just imagine what we could achieve if we all knew what each one of us knows.

John Browne
Group Chief Executive, BP
January 2001

PREFACE

'Deliver more, and do it with less resources.'

Isn't that the productivity challenge that everyone in business is facing today?

A key way to achieve this is by sharing know-how – by using and adapting what someone else has already learned. Many people know instinctively they should be doing this, but struggle to know how to get started.

'How can I know enough not to be foolish – or to be fooled by someone else?'

Today, no one is, nor can be, an expert in everything. In every challenge, it is easy to feel that you don't know enough to keep up with the accelerating pace of change inside our organisations, let alone the world outside.

Start with the assumption that somebody somewhere has already done what you are trying to do. How can you find out whom, and learn from them?

You can read any number of excellent books on the theory of knowledge management. This one demonstrates how to put theory into practice, sharing the tools used and the experience and insights gained of two leading practitioners working within BP.

So why are two people from BP writing this book? We felt it is a story worth telling. We have learned a lot through our journey of discovery and continue to do so. We want to share some of what we have learned with you, and we want to stimulate you to learn and apply what you have learned in order to become ever more productive. We have written half of the chapters each, which may account for any slight differences in style and stories. The book tells of our experience of knowledge management, the tools and techniques we have found useful, what we have done to create the right environment and how it has evolved.

It is a practical, pragmatic workbook *full* of hints and tips to help people make their very next steps.

You won't find too much theory here. Rather it is a book about what we have practised and what we have learned from practising it. We are writing it in our "spare time" because we are busy putting knowledge management into action. It is the story of how we have applied it in our own context that is within BP, one of the world's largest organisations. By comparing this with your own experiences, in your own context, we know you will be able to adapt what you do to be more effective. We have used the tools and techniques in a variety of businesses – large and small. Others are applying them successfully in different organisations – charities, government organisations and other business sectors. We are confident that the principles, the model and the tools are scalable and transferable. But don't take our word for it. Read on.

How can you get the best out of this book?

The book has been laid out in a style to emulate web pages in order to make it easier for the reader to focus on what they want to know, rather than what we, the authors want to tell them. There are links between pages so if you are following a certain line of thinking you can follow that directly to relevant knowledge. Alternatively the book can be read conventionally. The chapters include facilitator's notes, and action zones highlighted by the following icon.

At the action zones, take a pause in your reading and start doing something applicable to your own situation.

Part 1 of the book provides an overview. It sets the context, defines knowledge management, provides a model to use and describes the environment for successful knowledge management. In short it provides the basis to get started.

Part 2 of the book describes how we have applied a number of tools and techniques to help us manage knowledge. They help us learn before, during and after everything we do. They help us get in touch with people who know, and to develop communities who act as guardians of the company's knowledge.

Part 3 looks at how we are embedding the principles within company-wide processes and where we aim to go next.

At the back we've included some resources to help you get started.

Read the chapters relevant to you, compare it with your own experience and do something different. Then reflect and learn from what you have done. If someone comes to us and says "I read your book and applied some of the ideas. This is how my business has improved as a consequence," then we will feel the time spent preparing this book has been worthwhile.

So whether you want to know what knowledge management is about, wonder how to take the important next steps, or just want to hear how one company has successfully applied it, this book will appeal to you.

It is a book for the business person, the business student, the public servant, the educationalist, and information professional.

Finally, this is a record of what we know at a single point in time, now. Our world continues to change, and we continue to learn. We look forward to hearing what you learn through the experience of reading, and most importantly *applying*, what follows in this book. For details of how to contact us, please refer to the Resources section (pp. 205–14) at the back of the book.

ACKNOWLEDGEMENTS

While exploring knowledge management, we have learned a lot. We have learned from a great range of people both inside and outside BP, too many to mention, in some cases too many to remember, and in a few cases too many to be aware of. We have learned from people in our businesses applying the principles, tools and techniques in their own context, and generating the stories and quotes that you will find throughout the book. It is only because many people have *really applied* knowledge management in BP, that we were motivated to write this book. Theory doesn't excite us but business results, as a consequence of the application of knowledge management, do.

We will single out BP's Knowledge Management Team led by Kent Greenes, with whom we laughed, cried and learned much together. This team worked tirelessly for two years to fan flames, and light new fires across the company – fires that have spread and are still burning brightly today. The other team members were Neil Ashton, Catherine Day, Gareth Edwards, Tony Kuhel, Nick Milton, Walt Palen, Keith Pearse, Barry Smale, Dave Wolstenholme and Tom Young.

Additionally, we wish to recognise the Drilling Learning Team for their early pioneering work in knowledge management, and more recently, the Operations Excellence Team, who have embedded knowledge sharing into daily business of thousands of operations staff.

We are grateful to Barry Smale and Phil Forth for their thoroughness in critiquing the book in its draft form, and for providing their suggestions for improvement so rapidly.

Finally, we are indebted to our wives, Louise and Stella for supporting, encouraging, sacrificing, reviewing, challenging, uplifting and at times, gently deflating our egos!

Chris Collison and Geoff Parcell

December 2000

Part

Overview

1

SETTING THE CONTEXT

1

Have a read of this chapter to set the context for the rest of the book. In it we describe what each chapter is about in order to help you navigate your way around. So whether you want to get an overview of knowledge management, or whether you want some tools or techniques that you can apply, or you want to know what BP is currently doing with knowledge management, you'll learn exactly where to go.

We've just finished dealing with a kitchen design engineer. We want to improve our kitchen layout. We spend a lot of time in the kitchen and although its functional, it could be turned into something altogether more efficient and have a better ambience. So we have called in an expert. How can we ascertain whether this person knows what they are talking about, and whether what they are proposing is absolutely necessary, fits our body shapes and is in our interests rather than lining the pockets of the engineer?

The simple answer is we can't, we have to trust the expert. But how can we trust an engineer who only crossed the threshold 15 minutes ago? We can begin by asking a few simple questions and listen to the response we get; not only to the content of the response but also the way he delivers it. Is he talking down to us, or talking in technical terms and acronyms that we don't understand? Or is he pitching it at a level we can understand and checking for our understanding? Is he telling us stories to demonstrate a point and at the same time demonstrating his track record?

How do you trust an expert?

'I did a job for a television presenter in Maidenhead recently and she had a built in microwave, a fridge with slide out drawers and a fantastic cooking hob in the round. She was ecstatic. Not only was preparing quick meals for the family simplified, she could also entertain dinner guests in the kitchen whilst she was finishing the cooking. And do you know what her favourite dish was?'

What of his appearance? He is dressed smartly to show some respect, but has hands that have clearly been used to manual work. He has the tools of his trade about him, a measure, a pencil and pad, and a screwdriver to prod at the plaster. What does that tell us about the quality of the job he is likely to do?

This is the third engineer we've invited round to quote. We looked for a selection from the Yellow Pages® telephone directory, all work locally and each offers something different. As well as being able to compare the prices for the job, we are learning better questions to ask and also what differentiates their service and their products. Now which one shall we choose?

Increasingly each of us is being asked to be accountable for more and more both at work and in our private lives. Who suffers if the kitchen is not installed properly? We do. We have to keep out of the kitchen for a while longer and the family complains. We learn all the time; *we learn what questions to ask so that when the time is right we make the right decision.*

Start by asking simple questions

The authors were part of a team who got started in knowledge management by asking simple questions of others both inside and outside their organisation, BP. As we developed confidence in ourselves and inspired confidence in others that they could make a difference, we had a real impact on business performance. Once you have sorted out what you know and what you need to know, it's easy to ask a question to fill the gap in your knowledge.

BP is a multinational company of 100,000 people involved in:

- exploration for, and production of, oil and gas;

- refining of crude oil;

- the marketing of gasoline, lubricants and aviation fuel;

- the manufacture and sales of petro-chemicals;

- gas production, distribution and sales;

- power generation; and

- solar and renewable sources of energy.

BP is also socially and environmentally responsible and makes money for its shareholders. The company is headed by Sir John Browne, who believes that sharing what we know drives improved business performance. BP is divided into 150 businesses, some with as few as 50 people. We have learned that the principles of knowledge management can be adapted to any size of business.

One of the first projects we worked on was in Vietnam. BP has a business there developing a project to produce gas from the South China Sea, and deliver it onshore where it is converted to electricity to support the country's growing power requirement. The business had been made aware of knowledge management at a time when negotiations with the Vietnamese government had broken down, and they were prepared to try anything once.

We flew in to Ho Chi Minh City with Ed Guthrie, a retired US Army Colonel, without any clear idea of the problem or of how we might solve it. And we were the experts!

We asked a simple question, 'What is the main issue you have to deal with?' We asked that of a large number of people in the organisation for the first three days. There were different views on what the issue was, each person seeing the issue from their own particular stance. By reviewing the responses we got, we were able to pose more focused questions to understand the issues better. Ed noticed the parallels between the US Army's approach and BP's approach to Vietnam.

'What is the main issue you have to deal with?'

'You came here for one reason, looking for a big oilfield. Yet when you found something different, gas, you didn't change your tactics,

*your approach. You wanted the Vietnamese to follow your way of
doing business. That's just like us (The US Army). We came into
this country, in the 60s for one reason. What we found was rather
different. They didn't operate to our rules.'*

This is where transferring best practice comes unstuck so often.
Rarely can something that has worked well in one location and in
one situation be applied directly to another. The solution often
disappoints. In this book we'll share with you some real examples
and ask you to consider whether they are useful for you to adapt into
your own context. We've always struggled with the question, who
can define good practice? We believe it is the person who uses the
practice next, who determines whether it makes a difference to what
they are doing.

Many books have been written on the subject of knowledge management. We have presented to many businesses on the topic. Yet often
people come along and say 'Now what do I have to do to actually
get started?'

**Getting
started … you
are already
doing it!**

Let us tell you the first secret … you are already doing
it! In fact, it's more difficult not to do it. Each of us has
everyday encounters where we want to find out something
extra from someone who knows more. 'What's the best
way of getting a train into London?' 'If I'm thinking of going to
Disney World in April, what is the best option?' I'm going to get a
new kitchen fitted? What are the things I need to know about? What
have I forgotten?

In today's world, getting into action fast gives us a sense of progress,
but if it's the wrong task or a task done in the wrong order, we may
be wasting our resources by doing the wrong thing. Far better then
to do the research before you start, talk to people who
have already done it or had it done. Pause too, at regular
intervals, to reflect on what has happened so far and how
that might modify what you do in future. At the end, take
time to review what was actually achieved versus what you
had planned for at the outset. Learning before, learning
during and learning after is a key principle of knowledge
management. Taking the time to learn in order to make the time to
do will lead to better results.

**Learning
before,
learning
during and
learning after**

Just think for a moment about the last time you purchased, leased or ordered a car. Did you spare it much thought? Or did you go to the first car dealer and select one? Each of us has a different preferred buying strategy. I spend time doing some research for mine. My preferences may have been triggered by an advertisement in a magazine or on TV. I may have admired a friend's or colleague's car; even had a ride in it one lunchtime. Can you recall how you started?

Like the time you bought a car

I then read reviews and comparisons in car magazines. For me this is the fun part, looking at a spreadsheet of criteria that compares the acceleration from 0–60mph, the engine size, and the storage capacity in cubic litres. I then visit a few showrooms to stroke the bodywork, feel the seats and test-drive a limited number of models. I adjust the driver's seat and steering wheel to my satisfaction; listen to the sound of the engine accelerating, and block out the sales patter of the over-eager salesman. I then go away to think about it for a while, talk it through with my loved one, and ask advice from colleagues driving a similar car, perhaps ask a mechanic. But what finally convinces me?

> *Stop here* and think about how you went about your last car purchase. How did you choose what you bought? And what finally convinced you to part with your money or signature?

Now, how often do you put that much effort into making a business decision at work?

What we describe in this book is a model for the environment we work within. It is a model that can be applicable to any organisation. We've made links between pages, so if you are following a certain line of thinking you can follow that directly to relevant knowledge. Alternatively the book can be read conventionally from start to finish.

Navigating through the book

Would a bit more detail help you decide where to start? If not, go straight page 11. These are the thirteen chapters with a paragraph about each. The first five provide an overview. The next six describe practical tools and techniques, applicable in any size organisation. Then there is a chapter describing where BP currently is in applying these tools and techniques to drive business performance. Finally we review, to know better next time.

1. *Setting the context.* This describes what the book is about and how it is set out, to enable you to navigate the knowledge quickly.

2. *What is knowledge management? And what isn't it?* Knowledge management has proved very difficult to define. It is about capturing, creating, distilling, sharing and using know-how. That know-how includes explicit and tacit knowledge. Know-how is used as shorthand for know-how, know-what, know-who, know-why and know-when. It's not about books of wisdom and best practices, its more about the communities that keep know-how of a topic alive by sharing what they know, building on it and adapting it to their own use. It is not a snapshot of what is known at a single point in time, but an evolving set of know-how kept current by people who regularly use it.

What is knowledge management?

3. *The holistic model – it's more than the sum of the parts.* To make a real difference in delivering results through sharing know-how, it is important to work every element of a process model. The model describes how to turn business objectives into results by learning before, learning during and learning after. It also requires tapping into and feeding the know-how of the community and network and recognising that knowledge is more than a book of wisdom of best practices.

Apply it holistically

By applying the model consistently and persistently the authors know business results will improve.

4. *Getting the environment right.* One of the most difficult things to do in today's business environment appears to be to request help. People fear that requesting help is an acknowledgement that the requestor is not up to the task. Setting the environment up so that it is OK to ask for some assistance from peers is key. Inside BP, there is no doubt that one big enabler was to create an infrastructure of common machines and versions of software networked across the globe. This offered the potential to share, but did not guarantee the delivery of the business results. Getting the right processes in place and accessing the people with the right behaviours was key to delivery.

Ask for help

5. *Getting started – just do it.* Understanding what knowledge management is about intellectually is a first step. Understanding that the model has several components, each of which must be worked on, is helpful. Procrastinating takes it *Ask a simple* no further. We learned to just get started by working *question* on something simple. It could be as simple as asking a question – 'What is the key issue for this business?' – then listening carefully to, collecting and distilling, the responses to play back. As long as there are regular reviews to check and adjust your activity, the shared learning will begin at once.

OK that sets the scene. Now lets look at some of those tools and techniques.

6. *Learning from your peers – somebody has already done it.* Peer assists are a technique to learn early on in the doing phase – a kind of project-design meeting if you like. It's about sharing what people know in their own context, then sharing this with others who share what they know in their context. *Learn before* Knowing what is generic, and what the differences are, enables people to create future possibilities together, which can be firmed into options and then action. Learning is not complete until a different action has been taken as a consequence.

7. *Learning whilst doing – time to reflect.* A technique learned from the US Army is called After Action Review (AAR). As well as quickly learning from the last event, so that it can be applied to the next, it is also a means of building a *Learn during* stronger team. It is simple to do, flexible, and when applied consistently, effective. In the US army they do it anywhere, including on the back of a truck after a skirmish with the enemy!

8. *Learning after doing – when it's all over.* At the end of a project, or distinct change, sit down with all the people with a stake in the result and review what went well and what could have been done differently. Consider who can benefit from *Learn after* what has been learned? Identify a customer for the knowledge. Recount specific examples and focus on the activity rather than imply blame. Consider what you would do differently if you were to do it over again. Ask the customer what they have learned from this review; their insights may well be different,

as they have a different set of experiences to filter the messages through.

9. *Finding the right people – if only I knew who.* Key to learning what others have done is to know who to ask, and being able to reach them easily. Know-how is organically held by the community or network and constantly reused, revised, adapted and distilled. Key to knowing who, and being able to reach them, is a Yellow Pages or index of people's skills, experiences and contact details.

Get hold of the people who know

10. *Networking and communities of practice.* People with common interests or discipline practices frequently form networks, or communities of practice, to share their know-how, either to improve the capability of each individual to do his or her job better, or to deliver on a common goal or objective. These networks sometimes meet face to face but more often make use of a multitude of technology aids to collaborate virtually.

Become a node on the network

11. *Leveraging what we've learned – capturing knowledge.* It is important to find a way of capturing what has been learned, in order that others can reuse it, sometimes immediately and otherwise after a distinct time lag. It is important to identify a customer for this captured knowledge or it is unlikely ever to be used again.

Capture and share good practices

What get captured at first are practices, sometimes these are shared and can be called common practices. What makes a *good* practice though and *who* can decide what is good? And how can we speed up the process of identifying the good practices?

12. *Embedding it in the organisation – preparing to let go.* You know when sharing knowledge has become an unconscious competence, when there are no longer people dedicated to knowledge management in the organisation, when the techniques are embedded in the core business processes. At BP, the focus has been on embedding them in company-wide, operational excellence processes, and in sharing project lessons to enhance capital productivity. People who are already busy no longer have to think about learning before, learning during and learning after. It is embedded in the way they do things.

Make it an unconscious competence

The next phase includes identifying the other core processes and embedding the tools of learning before, during, and after into them.

13. *Review of the book – what did we set out to do?* This chapter applies one of the key tools outlined in the book, the after action review. Let's review what we set out to do, what did we actually achieve? Why was there a difference and what can we learn from that? Our intent was to write a book that was both practical and pragmatic, to help people take their first steps to do something different in order that they could learn from that and adapt further. Did we achieve that, if not what was the difference and why was it different? What can we learn from that?

Apply what we have learned

So spend a few moments writing down three questions that occur to you. Having read this chapter, what do you most want to know next?

1. _____
   _____

2. _____
   _____

3. _____
   _____

Then decide which chapter to start with, or look in the index for the topic most appropriate to your questions.

Bon Voyage!

WHAT IS KNOWLEDGE MANAGEMENT?

In this chapter we discuss:

- Defining knowledge management – what it is, and isn't.

- Creating the environment.

- Components of knowledge management.

- Not just know-how but also know-why, know-who, know-when, know-what and know-where.

- Tacit versus explicit knowledge.

- From unconscious incompetence to unconscious competence.

'What did you do at work today, Daddy?'

How do I answer Martha, our three-year-old daughter, in a meaningful way? How do I summarise the manner in which I spend my day trying to align and simplify corporate activities, investigating collaborative technologies, encouraging people to capture and share lessons learned, facilitating discussions in networks, matchmaking between different parts of our business, developing intellectual capital strategy ...

Explaining knowledge management in simple terms

'Um.' (Thinks... How can I make this sound interesting?) 'I talked with some people on the telephone, sent some e-mails, read some stories on the computer, had some sandwiches, sent some more e-mails, helped some people to make friends with some other people and then came home to you and Mummy' (Did that sound interesting?)

'What sandwiches did you have?' (Clearly not!)

Whether to peers at the office, close friends or inquisitive children, knowledge management has never been particularly easy to describe, define or explain. It's not a great topic for parties either, in case you've ever tried!

Defining knowledge management

One of our favourite definitions comes from Arian Ward, of Work Frontiers International:

'It's not about creating an encyclopaedia that captures everything that anybody ever knew. Rather, it's about keeping track of those who know the recipe, and nurturing the culture and the technology that will get them talking.'

Get the right people talking This shifts the emphasis from the creation of vast knowledge repositories, and places the higher value on the knowledge in people's heads and finding ways to increase its mobility.

- Have you ever had the feeling that someone just must have done this before, but you don't know who or where to find him or her?

- Have you ever had a chance encounter at the water cooler and learned a piece of information just in time to influence what you were doing?

We have.

Larry Prusak of IBM speaks of a continuum of knowledge ranging from 'capture' at one end to 'connectivity' at the other.

Capture   Connectivity

A focus on capture drives a set of activities relating to codi-   *It's a range of*
fication of knowledge. Organisations such as the US Army   *activities*
serve as good examples of this approach, investing large
efforts in creating and distributing explicit knowledge – information
packs, briefing notes and knowledge bases, and websites – all with
tremendous efficiency.

An alternative approach is to invest time and energy in the processes
and technologies which stimulate connections between people. This
could involve the creation of communities and networks, peer interactions, workshops, collaboration tools and knowledge directories.
These connections and conversations in turn address the transfer
of tacit knowledge. This is the knowledge locked up in the heads
of individuals that tends not ever to be written down, but flows
between staff sharing war stories at a bar, or when a member of staff
is mentored by another.

These two extremes illustrate the range of options available. Neither
one is right or wrong; the selection of a point on the spectrum should
simply be a reflection of the culture in an organisation at a point in
time. Some point on that spectrum represents the best return on your
knowledge management investment.

Take a minute or two to consider this.

Where is the largest prize for your organisation? At
which point on the spectrum should you invest your
effort? What is the right balance for you?

Over the past few years, BP's position has been biased towards the
'connectivity' end of the spectrum, although some focused *knowledge
capture* also formed an important part of our approach, where the
subject matter is of strategic importance.

Tacit versus explicit

Knowledge can be held in people's heads (we call this tacit knowledge) or it can be written down (explicit knowledge). It is not possible to capture the full richness of what's in people's heads. If you don't believe us, try writing down your knowledge of how to ride a bicycle!

It's in people's heads

On the other hand explicit knowledge can be stored and searched, and can be a good catalyst for connecting people together. Then, questioning can bring out the tacit knowledge.

A way of thinking about capture and connectivity is to consider the relationship between 'what do others know' and 'what info do we have.' The following diagram illustrates this:

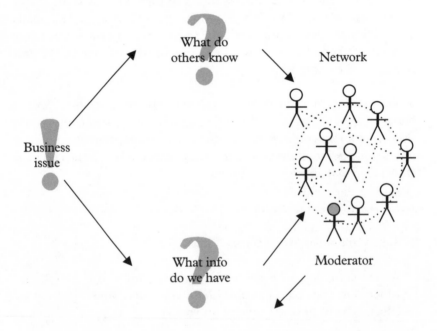

Think about one of your important business issues – perhaps it's a need to expand sales, recruit the right people or retain customers.

As you think about this issue, there will be two routes that you might take in seeking out knowledge.

... and it's written down

- One is looking for 'what do others know,' and searching them out and talking with them directly – this often leads to a network of other leads and contacts, or a community of practice.

- Another is to seek out 'what is known' – what has already been captured or written down that I could make use of?

The weakness of the second approach for us has been that once captured, knowledge grows stale unless there is some mechanism for refreshing it. Some would go further and maintain that a document cannot contain knowledge but only information. The information triggers thoughts, which you compare with your memory of past experiences. This in turn enables understanding.

Our experience is that to be useful knowledge needs to be refreshed frequently and it takes the organic nature of a network to own and refresh the knowledge with new experiences.

it needs refreshing

Perhaps this is why companies that sell mineral water market their products as 'natural spring water' and 'bottled directly at the source.' When was the last time you bought mineral water that was 'drawn from the lake?'

In the diagram above, the mechanism for refreshing 'what info do we have' is where the moderator of the network takes responsibility for maintaining and updating the body of knowledge – closing the loop.

A hybrid science – or is it an art?

Get a balance of people, process and technology

Knowledge management is a hybrid discipline, neither art nor science; functionally it can straddle the fields of learning and organisational development, human resources and IT. This overlap is often represented as three circles. Knowledge management is the area where the three circles overlap:

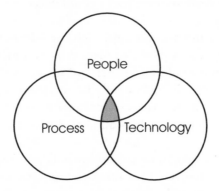

The messages in this model are powerful. The elements for successful knowledge management include:

- a common, reliable *technology* infrastructure to facilitate sharing;

- connecting the *people* who know, and the behaviours to ask, listen and share; and

- some *processes* to simplify sharing, validation, distillation.

All too often we embark on a change programme, and concentrate energy disproportionately on one, or possibly two of the circles. If we focus on people and technology, but neglect to consider process, then we risk automating the past.

Technology and process together are powerful partners, but without the people aspect, there is a strong risk that any effort to make change will generate resistance.

Finally, by considering people and process, but neglecting technology, we fail to capitalise on the power that IT brings to make explicit knowledge globally accessible, and, through multimedia and video-conferencing, to make tacit knowledge more widely available.

The activities of managing knowledge

There is a large marketplace for knowledge management products and techniques; your in-tray is probably full of them. Software companies will sell you the latest collaboration and search tools, consultancies will sell you learning processes, and journalists will sell you their services for capturing corporate history.

Whilst these components can all be valuable in isolation, we believe that the greatest value is generated when these pieces of the puzzle come together in a complementary way. *If you know the picture that you are trying to create, it is easier to spot the gaps.* Knowledge can be created, discovered, captured, shared, distilled, validated, transferred, adopted, adapted and applied. Starting with a business activity, the first step is to use a learning process to reflect on what happened, and draw out the lessons learned.

Create, discover, capture

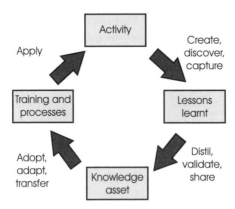

Whilst it is great to capture lessons, a huge database of these can become wearisome to navigate. Our experience is that finding a way to distil the key points from these lessons and capturing them as a more concentrated 'knowledge asset' is far more helpful for people.

Distil, validate, share

Adapt, adopt, transfer, apply However, there's no guarantee that people will actually refer to these, unless there is some way of transferring and embedding these key learning points into the training materials and business processes that staff use. Then the knowledge actually becomes applied, and something changes.

Let's face it – if nothing changes, then knowledge management is unlikely to impact your bottom line.

What do we mean when we talk about knowledge?

OK, so if defining knowledge management is difficult maybe defining knowledge is more straightforward?

It is very common to see a blurring of the meaning of data, information and knowledge. Over recent years, databases have been re-cast as more fashionable 'knowledge bases' in order to appeal to the marketplace. They are closely related and we have found it useful to make some distinctions.

When I travel to Boston I get the following *data* from our travel office on an e-mail: AA79 21st August Dep:13:45 Arr: 15:30. Fine. But in order to get there I could use a bit more *information.* The plane leaves from Terminal 4 at Heathrow and there is a business-class lounge which I can use. By talking with some colleagues who travel to Boston regularly I *know* that it is possible to request an upgrade to first class, that I can use a fast track through customs and that the plane generally arrives ahead of schedule.

Knowledge is richer than data or information The knowledge I now have is related to the data but much richer and enables me to make some decisions. Of course I have to trust those colleagues in order to put some confidence in their knowledge.

The Concise Oxford Dictionary defines knowledge as 'familiarity gained by experience.' Sometimes we need to experience it ourselves to know. At other times it is sufficient that someone else, who has experienced it, shares that experience with us. Whether or not you act, based on someone else's experience, will depend on how well you know and trust them.

People sometimes interchange the terms 'know-how' and 'knowledge,' but there is a danger that in doing so we miss some other important attributes of what could be considered as knowledge.

Know-how is the processes, procedures, techniques and tools you use to get something done.

Know-why relates to strategic insight – understanding the context of your role, and the value of your actions. It's the 'big picture' view of things. Think back to your first ever job. Did anyone explain to you why what you did was important, or were you just expected to 'get on with it' and not ask stupid questions? Know-why is a key to lifting morale and generating commitment from staff.

> *It's more than know-how – it's know-why, know-what, know-who, know-where, and know-when.*

Know-what is the activities required to complete a task, it's the information needed in order to take a decision and it's the things you need to collect together before making something.

Know-who includes knowledge about relationships, contacts, networks, who to call on for help. It's the 'I know a man who can' factor. All of us apply and build up this type of knowledge on a day-to-day basis, often subconsciously. If your role is sales-oriented, you'll know just how important know-who can be.

Know-where is that uncanny ability that some people have for navigating through and finding the right information. You probably know people in your office who fulfil this role, functioning like human search engines. If you visit Yahoo!, or one of the other major Internet portals, you'll be in a knowledge-rich environment where most of the content is know-where – links to where relevant *know-how* can be found on the Internet.

Know-when is the sense of timing – to know the best time to do something, to make a decision, or to stop something.

Is 'knowledge management' the best label?

Despite the term being something of an oxymoron, we used the term 'knowledge management' to describe the area in which we are working. Some people have taken issue with us over the term and

Choose the best words to describe what you do

somehow feel threatened by the suggestion that someone wants to take control of their knowledge. 'Performance through learning,' 'organisational learning,' 'shared learning,' 'shared knowledge' or simply 'working smarter' could be used. It's worth investing time up front with people from your organisation to select the most appropriate term. The wrong words could get in the way. Perhaps you don't need a label at all.

Creating the environment

It's like herding cats

I once heard knowledge management likened to herding cats. Stop for a minute and imagine yourself in a large room – or even a field – full of cats, trying to herd them towards one corner.

Not going well, is it? So if you can't *herd* cats, how could you get them to do what you want? You might suggest providing scratching-posts, saucers of milk, warm fires and balls of wool – components that go to make up the right environment.

... so get the environment right

That's exactly the view we took when thinking about knowledge management. You can't manage knowledge – nobody can. What you can do is to manage the environment in which knowledge can be created, discovered, captured, shared, distilled, validated, transferred, adopted, adapted and applied.

In order to create an environment within which knowledge rapidly flourishes we need:

- *the right conditions*: a common reliable infrastructure and an organisation willing be entrepreneurial;

- *the right means*: a common model, tools and processes; and

- *the right actions*: where people instinctively seek, share and use knowledge.

Knowledge management as an unconscious competence

If you go into the rest rooms in many of BP's offices and look in the mirror you'll see a sticker that reads, 'You are looking at your Safety Officer.' It makes a good point. We have worked many years to embed the concept of safety management into the workforce – to spread the message that safety is everyone's responsibility, not just the responsibility of your manager or a central function.

Sustainable knowledge management

Knowledge management can be approached in a similar way – the ideal outcome is that people manage knowledge as part of their daily business without thinking of it as an extra task, and that the leadership of the company and the company processes reinforce this.

The following four steps illustrate this point.

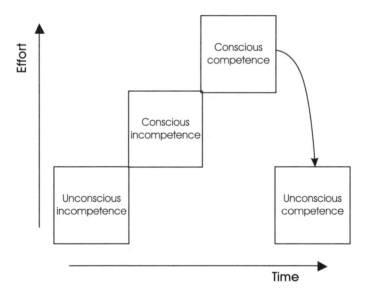

Start at the bottom left corner – *unconscious incompetence*. This first box is the 'ignorance is bliss' section. Perhaps as an organisation, you aren't good at managing knowledge, but it has never occurred to you that it was a problem, or that this is something that should concern you.

My wife Louise taught me to drive when we'd been going out together for about six months. When I started driving, I had a bad habit of 'grating the gears,' but I was oblivious to that fact – unconsciously incompetent.

Moving to the next step, this is when light dawns – as an organisation, you become aware that you *are* failing to manage knowledge effectively, and that you need to take action. This is *conscious incompetence.*

'Do you know that you always do that?' Louise said to me during driving lesson number three. 'You always grate the gears. You keep missing third.' Once my fragile ego had recovered, and I'd finished blaming the gearbox, I had to admit that she was right. I'd become consciously incompetent – progress!

The third step is where you deliberately focus your efforts. Having identified a gap in your capability as a company, you implement a programme, or initiative, to raise awareness and provide the relevant tools and resources for the businesses to be able to demonstrate improvement. This is *conscious competence.*

Conscious competence requires effort

'Right, pull over and switch the engine off!' Still on lesson three, and still grating the gears. Louise had had enough. 'Close your eyes. Put down the clutch. Start in first, that's right. Second, over to third, then fourth. Now again.' After five minutes of 'blind gear changes,' I'd got it. Success every time provided I thought about it. I'd become consciously competent.

The last box is where you are aiming for as an organisation. Your staff instinctively share knowledge; and learning before, during and after any event is the norm. They don't pick up the telephone and ask a consultant for advice – managing knowledge has become second nature. This is *unconscious competence.* At this stage the knowledge is tacit. You have to be questioned to consider how you do it. BP hasn't arrived here yet, certainly not across all of its business units – it remains our aspiration.

... but unconscious competence is the goal

After lesson five, I made it – unconsciously competent. Painless gear changes just 'happened,' and I selected the right gear instinctively. I had become an expert!

This four-step model can be used to describe the stages for embedding knowledge management in BP.

We started by listening to what was already going on inside the organisation, and identifying successful examples. For example, the drilling team in the Gulf of Mexico who had built an unprecedented *three days* for reflection and learning into their project plans, and saved millions of dollars with every well that they drilled as a result. Stories like these were told around the company as implicit challenges to the way other businesses operated – awakening them to their unconscious incompetence.

As we learned more of what was going on inside and outside the company, we began to create some models to describe knowledge management, and tried to focus the diverse set of tools and processes into a few key ones – tools for learning before, during and after an event. These tools helped to raise the level of competence in different parts of the company, from Japan to Alaska, as members of a small central team of internal consultants worked with business teams to transfer the skills and thereby demonstrate the real-world relevance of this particular management buzzword.

One team member worked on a project to construct *self-service* retail sites in Japan, something that had never been done before in that part of the world. Another member worked with refinery operators to improve their ability to shut down and recommission the plant in record time.

These projects in turn generated their own success stories, and began to spread the word at the grass-roots level, that knowledge management was relevant, and that these tools and techniques had real, bottom-line impact. A series of fires had been lit across the company.

Success breeds success

The final phase – the one which we're still working in – is what happens after the initiative phase is over, when the message has been heard by most, understood by many and applied by some. Shortly after the BP-Amoco merger, the central knowledge-management function was disbanded, and the emphasis placed on embedding the all-important KM principles into the company's core processes. Growing closer to unconscious competence, the organisation is putting knowledge management practices into its everyday business activity, and embedding the lessons.

Processes which institutionalise KM principles

We couldn't find any way of moving directly from unconscious incompetence to unconscious competence – we found that implementation of any programme requires time to be spent in all four steps. We are working hard to reduce the time to competency. The approach we took is summarised in the five points below:

- Look for what's already going on inside the company. Find some heroes.

- Check the external world for good practices and test them inside the organisation.

- Focus on a few key tools and promote them. Make it simple and avoid creating a new language.

- Work in depth in a few critical areas to prove the value.

- Look to the existing company processes and 'infect them' with knowledge management principles.

So, knowledge management is about connecting to those who know the recipe more than capturing an encyclopaedia of knowledge. Knowledge itself can be held in people's heads and it can be written down. Both sources should be used. It's about striking the right balance of people, process and technology. Knowledge is not just captured or shared, it is also created, discovered, distilled, validated, transferred, adopted, adapted and applied. Knowledge is richer than data and information; it's about familiarity gained from experience.

It's difficult to manage knowledge, but you can create and nurture the environment for knowledge sharing to flourish. The aim is for knowledge management to become an unconscious competence.

The next chapter moves on from these definitions and descriptions into a model that can be applied to any business situation. Fasten your seatbelt!

THE HOLISTIC MODEL
– IT'S MORE THAN
THE SUM OF THE PARTS

So now we know what knowledge management is and isn't, what can we do? In this chapter we discuss:

- Using a model to provide a framework.

- Turning business objectives into business results.

- Learning before, during and after.

- Accessing and applying the know-how of the community.

- Making use of all parts of the model.

- Applying the model consistently.

It was 11.30 p.m. on a dark autumn night. John and Rachel were just returning home from a night out at the theatre. On turning a sharp bend in the road, they saw car headlights shining upwards at a crazy angle somewhere just off the road to the right of them. Then, they noticed a fresh gap in the wooden fence. John stopped the car, put on his hazard flashers, and rushed through the gap in the fence and across a ploughed field, with Rachel in pursuit.

A hundred metres into the field was a car with a single occupant half out of the car. John quickly took charge and despatched Rachel back to the car to drive to the nearest village to phone for an ambulance. He asked her to get the first aid kit and a torch from the rear of their Mercedes.

John noticed the badly distorted leg of the driver, hanging awkwardly from the car. He cursed Rachel for having driven off before coming back with the first-aid kit and torch. With a brief shiver he removed his own shirt, quickly put his jacket back on, and tore the shirt into strips to make a bandage. Clearly this was no time to wait or worry about what Rachel would say about his shirt. He struggled to recall what his first-aid training had been, some 15 years previously, then pulled the leg straight before tying two ankles together, to keep the tension on the broken leg. He then applied a further bandage to stem the flow of bleeding.

It was then he smelled the leaking fuel, and decided to drag the occupant from the car to a safer spot, away from the risk of fire. He struggled to undo the safety belt in the distorted cabin, but then dragged the casualty away across the muddy field. By the time he had moved 25 metres from the car he was feeling exhausted and slumped down by the casualty.

He saw the blue flashing light before he heard the siren. His wife was still not back. He rushed to meet the accident crew, flushed with pride that he had immobilised the leg.

The accident crew checked for pulse and circulation. There was none – the driver had died in the crash.

What has this to do with knowledge management? If John had a model in mind he would have checked the casualty's overall health. The Red Cross teaches the ABC model – Airways, Breathing, Circulation as the first checks on a casualty.

Why are models helpful?

Knowledge management is a complex area, and one which spans boundaries – learning and development, information technology, human resources. Having a model that describes the scope of activity that your knowledge management efforts cover, can be a powerful way to both monitor and communicate what your approach encompasses.

As a team, we spent several meetings and many, many discarded flipcharts before arriving at the model that follows. Our model relates learning processes, and the capture and transfer of knowledge to day-to-day business. Once we had a common view, it enabled us to identify any gaps or shortcomings in our approach, and to take steps to address them.

The power of a common view

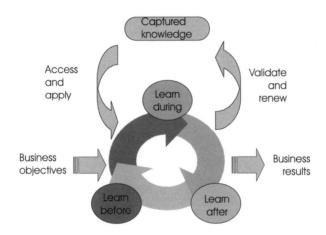

Whilst any step in isolation will make some difference, the real benefit will come from applying knowledge management holistically. This ensures that the end result is greater than the sum of its parts, and that the learning process is sustained. In the last chapter we described how the *framework* includes discovering, capturing, adapting, adopting, distilling, validating, sharing, and applying knowledge. It embraces people, process, and technology with equal importance. In order to excel at sharing what we know, and to capture meaningful knowledge, we require a common framework and the right set of skills.

One powerful example, that so impressed BP that they used it as part of their corporate advertising campaign, was the approach to the Development Drilling programme on Schiehallion oil field, north of Scotland.

> 'The capture and transfer of know-how from the Foinaven (north of Scotland) and Gulf of Mexico assets was a major factor in reducing the planned development costs by $50 million.'
>
> Development manager

Reusing knowledge is faster than recreating it. We have seen from people's experience that teams can 'have the time to halve the time', and use this increased productivity to create the space to share and learn more. By concentrating on what you need to *know*, then finding out the best way to learn it before focusing on what we need to *do*, the outcome is achieved faster and with less effort.

At the highest level, most companies work by setting business objectives for their staff, who in turn use knowledge to deliver business results. The first question we asked was:

'How can knowledge management make a difference in this simple process of getting business results from business objectives?'

Learning before, during and after

We believed that the key to this was to introduce learning at every opportunity. The first part of the holistic model is to ensure we learn *before*, *during* and *after* everything we do.

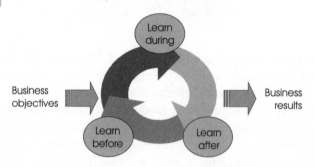

- *Learning before.* If we are about to start a task, it is likely that someone, inside or outside the company has done something similar before. *Why are we doing this? Are we sure we are setting off on the right activity? What can be learned from them? If we can reuse some knowledge, will this save us time to concentrate on activities that have not been undertaken before?*

- *Learning during.* Is what we have been doing likely to achieve our desired outcome? What can we learn about *what* we have been doing and *how* we are doing it? Is what is happening what we intended? We do this when we want to continuously improve based on reviewing our actions to date. It is easy to become blinkered whilst in the middle of a project – everybody needs to 'come up for air' at times and reflect on what has already been achieved.

- *Learning after.* Most of our activities are not one-time events. When we do something again, *how* can we do it better than the last time, and *how* can we capture and share what we have learned? Who could make use of what we have learned? As an organisation we reviewed significant Joint Ventures and mergers with other companies to develop the capability for doing it again even more effectively.

Another key element of the holistic model is:

Captured knowledge

This means capturing know-how in such a way that it can be reused. Knowledge needs storing for reuse; you cannot just leave it in people's heads. If you can find an effective way to capture it for transfer, others can look for it and find it, and the know-how will stay in the corporation even if the staff leave. One of the best ways that we have found to store know-how for effective reuse is by building a knowledge asset (outlined in Chapter 11).

There needs to be a link between the learning before/during/after circle and the knowledge itself, both to accessing what has already been captured and to capturing new knowledge. Networks and communities of practice are the primary route for enabling this access. We likened this to the way customers use a bank – making a withdrawal from a 'knowledge bank' at the start of a project and depositing new knowledge at the end.

Let's look at the elements in a little more detail.

Learn before doing

Typically we would learn before starting any new piece of work. Examples include entering a new market, assessing commercial options or, troubleshooting a manufacturing problem.

- It's likely someone has done this before. Make it the norm for any activity to find out what knowledge *is out there* before performing any piece of work.

- Try a search of your intranet or the Internet, using a search engine, or corporate Yellow Pages (see Chapter 9, Finding the Right People, p. 103) to find out where the experience lies in your company.

   In one example, a manager from BP Chemicals in SE Asia, searched for information on a particular fuel's additive; within five minutes he had found something on the company intranet in the US that was worth £10,000 to his business. As search technologies are steadily improving, becoming smarter, more precise and more proactive, examples like these should be on the increase.

- Put together a peer assist meeting, so that people with the knowledge can come and help with your problem. (See Chapter 6, p. 57 for more on peer assists.)

Learn during the activity

Routinely performed, 'learning during' activity will be of real benefit to team delivery.

- Learn from yourselves! Introduce simple techniques such as the After Action Review (AAR), a short team meeting to capture operational knowledge as you go (see Chapter 7, p. 75 for more on AARs). BP in Vietnam introduced AARs to learn how to negotiate with the Vietnamese, and ended up rethinking their negotiating strategy as a result.

- Learn from others. There are probably others out there facing similar problems to you on a day-to-day basis. Set up a community of practice – perhaps little more than a distribution list of interested parties – so you can tap into their know-how when you need it. (See Chapter 10, p. 123 for more on networks and communities.)

Learning after doing

A process of 'learning after doing' is valuable for the team, and helps them perform the next job better. It is also valuable for others who may face the same challenges that you have just faced, either immediately, or at some time in the future.

- Stop and hold a meeting so the team can reflect on what has happened. Even if you do not write anything down, you will carry the knowledge with you to the next project. However, writing it down is better. Putting knowledge into a searchable store is better still, since human memories fade unless backed up by something recorded.

- Hold a retrospect or some form of post-project appraisal in order to draw lessons and insights from those involved.

OK. So that tells you a bit about learning before, during and after everything we do. So where do we get knowledge from, where do we store it?

> **Captured knowledge**

Think of the difference between a magazine article and a text book. The magazine tells you just enough to get you interested, you can read it in ten minutes, all in one go. The article also gives references of where to go if you want to find out more.

Like a magazine article

Captured knowledge requires some context and also a collection of specific experiences that are 'distilled' to provide the content. BP labels such a collection a 'knowledge asset'. We found that this approach retains context as well as content, and provides the back-up material that someone may need in the future. We have learned that you do not have to write down everything you do, but capture the highlights and tell the story in a simple and engaging way.

It is vital to ask *who* knows, as well as *what* does the organisation know. In the earlier example of the Schiehallion oil field (see p.29), it was the drilling network that transferred the learning rapidly so the new team did not start at the bottom of the learning curve.

Even though we can capture knowledge, we cannot possibly capture everything. A lot of operational knowledge and experience will always remain in the heads of the practitioners, as tacit knowledge that we cannot codify easily. To make the best use of what BP knows, we build relationships with others who want to learn, and with those from whom we can learn. We call these sorts of knowledge-sharing groups 'networks' and 'communities'. They are the keys mechanisms for exchanging knowledge in BP. Some networks are formal and have clear objectives, while others are less formal (see chapter on networking, p. 123).

The final stage is to embed this captured knowledge into business processes. Knowledge is created from business activity, and needs to be embedded back into activity if it is to make a sustainable improvement to the business. In order to do this, the knowledge passes through a life cycle of a number of steps:

Embed captured knowledge back into the business process

- *Identify*, through some process of reflection, and pass into 'team history'.

- Analyse and *capture*, and draw out the lessons learned, record and package.

- After capturing enough experience, *validate* and distil the lessons into an approved set of guidelines – a knowledge asset.

- *Embed* these guidelines into the business process, so that they reach the people who need to use them.

- *Apply* and use them in business activity.

Capturing know-how is not sufficient on it's own. Far better if people already have a desire to give and to receive knowledge. Somehow you have to nurture the right behaviours and foster a supportive company culture. An example of supportive culture is one that recognises and rewards employees and teams for sharing and using learning in their day-to-day activities.

Learning tools, culture and behaviour – the 'chicken and egg' factor

A 'chicken and egg' factor works to reinforce this:

Learning tools and techniques can help create a favourable culture and sharing behaviours, and these behaviours and culture will be receptive to learning tools.

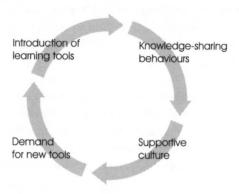

The trick is to start somewhere, and the virtuous circle will begin. Every employee in the organisation should be able to make some contribution to reinforcing this culture:

> *'In order to generate extraordinary value for shareholders, a company has to learn better than its competitors and apply that knowledge throughout its businesses faster and more widely than they do. The way we see it, anyone in the organisation who is not directly accountable for making a profit should be involved in creating and distributing knowledge that the company can use to make a profit.'*
>
> Sir John Browne, *Harvard Business Review*, 1997

So having established a model, how do you use it?

The entry point can be almost anywhere. It's possible to start with various elements of this model and extend to embrace the whole model. If you have just taken stock of where you are with your current project and want to know what next, use the holistic model as a template. Perhaps you should take what you've learned and build on a new or existing knowledge asset, or perhaps it prompts a request you can make of the network.

Finding the right place to start – anywhere!

In BP's Vietnam operations, the first step was to introduce AAR's to enable the business to review their progress with negotiations. Negotiations with host governments are often lengthy, complex and necessary before the company is prepared to make a large financial investment. The business was keen to try another tool. By using the model as a framework and marking the areas that were addressed, the learning before, during and after components could be 'ticked off' in turn.

Using the model as a checklist for KM activity

The model prompted the business leadership to consider who the community of practice (see chapter on networks, p. 123) was for their particular activity. Ten separate negotiations were ongoing but only four people in the business unit had an overview of all ten. Some issues were commercially sensitive so it made sense limiting that knowledge to a few – but more *could* be shared. The best exchange seemed to occur when everyone sat down for lunch together in the Hanoi office, hence the immediate community became all those involved in the ten negotiations, the management team and representatives from the local Vietnamese staff.

The business set up a 'war room' in Hanoi, a project room, a physical knowledge store in one of the offices. On the walls of this dedicated room, they pinned up charts made of the deal process, and of the structure of the Vietnam government organisation ... the 'stakeholder analysis'. People met in the room to prepare for meetings and to review the meetings. They had listed the key issues on the wall and they could discuss who they were seeing and the next steps in the negotiation. They could also discuss the interaction between different threads of the negotiation.

The Vietnam business captured a summary of the key AARs each week and reviewed them at the weekly management meeting. The management team used this in considering the priorities for the next negotiations.

How do we make this model add up to more than the sum of the parts?

We can see a result once people are using the tools of learning before, during and after, and are interacting with the store of knowledge, and the knowledge is being used and refreshed. The community of people interested in that knowledge feel responsible for keeping it current, they find it useful, and so they tap into it and learn before doing. They capture what they have learned and add it to the knowledge asset. They tidy up the store – remove unwanted or out-of-date knowledge and distil it so it is easy to reach the parts that make a difference. This generates a system which is reinforcing and self-sustaining.

Applying the model consistently

Reinforcing and sustaining
One of the biggest challenges we have faced is to stop people doing things differently each time. The nature of BP's operations has resulted in a strong engineering culture in which staff thrive on space to innovate – learning before is still a key step to innovating.

In the last chapter we explored the route to unconscious competence. At the earlier stage of conscious competence it is key to adopt a consistent approach in order to make it routine. Persisting with a model even when it doesn't work first time, or every time, is important.

For a golfer it's a bit like teaching your muscles how to swing the club properly. The pro gives you a set of points to think about before each swing of the club. At first you are thinking so hard about facing the club to the ball, getting your feet right, keeping your head down, taking the club back slowly that you miss the ball completely. Only once the pro distracts you does your unconscious take over and you hit the ball cleanly. It takes many months (did I hear you utter 'years'?) of practice for your muscles to learn the unnatural swing, so that it becomes an unconscious competence.

The idea of offering a model is to provide a consistent approach to managing knowledge so that a practitioner can repeat the approach several times until the 'muscles' are trained to do it naturally. At that stage the model can be dispensed with and the practitioner unconsciously applies the techniques.

So whilst learning to be competent, choose an approach and persistently stick to it. Once you are consciously competent then you can allow your unconscious to take over. At that stage being clear on your desired outcome (*knowing which way the green is, and how far it is*), and ensuring actions are consistent with getting you there (*selecting the appropriate club, bearing in mind where the bunkers are and how well you are playing today*) is probably more appropriate than always following the same approach.

> '*When we define where we want to be, all of our actions turn out to be congruent with that place.*'
>
> Phil Forth, consultant

Over the course of our implementation of knowledge management, we have developed this simple holistic model to use as a framework. At the end of the day, it is *only a model!*

We invite you to try it out in your own working environment. If the model serves to align and focus your actions, then it has value. If it leads to the creation of a different model then that is even better, and please let us know – we would love to hear from you.

The real business benefits come from working on all parts of the model and embedding the activities into the routine business processes. This develops a sustainable capability rather than an ongoing dependency on 'experts'.

GETTING THE ENVIRONMENT RIGHT

4

We've discussed what knowledge management is and proposed a model for framing it, but how do we create the right environment to make it happen?

In this chapter we discuss:

- Removing the barriers for information sharing.

- A common operating environment.

- The organisation of BP – peer processes.

- Processes to encourage sharing.

- Learning to ask for help.

- Active listening.

We are wondering how many of you have experienced the same embarrassment that we have? The embarrassment of the school dance. There we are in the school hall, which is camouflaged in bright decorations and balloons and the lights dimmed. The boys are at one end, close to where the soft drinks and refreshments are served. The girls, from the same co-educational school or

The embarrassment of the school dance

the local high school, cluster at the other near to the aspiring band from the school.

When the band takes a break and the recognisable rhythms emanate from the DJ's turntable many of the girls start dancing with each other. Eventually, usually only 30 minutes before the end of the evening, the bolder boys, perhaps encouraged by illicit refreshments, move in to claim a dance with their favourite girl of the evening. In some cases the girls do not wait and drag their dream man onto the floor.

The last slow dance fills the floor with hugging couples, whilst those around the periphery dream of what might have been. All too soon the harsh lights of the hall switch on, revealing the acne, and dampening the ardour of all but the most passionate of couples. And the environment is exposed for what it really is – the school hall.

For a few precious hours the organising committee have done a great job of removing the barriers to romance by converting the hall into an environment where romance can flourish.

So what are the barriers to creating an attractive environment for the sharing of know-how?

Understanding the barriers to sharing

Firstly there is the barrier of technology. I struggle to share a document electronically with you because you are not connected to my network. It could be because you don't use the same software as I do, or you have a more recent version of the software that does not recognise my version. Maybe I have mistyped your e-mail address, or the file is too large to send.

So I send you a floppy disk, or CD, with the document on. Perhaps I have compressed it to make sure I can get the figures included and you don't have the decompression software. Does any of this sound familiar to you?

Then there is the barrier of the business processes and the way we organise ourselves. Even within the same office we struggle to share something that would be useful to another department because we focus totally on the tasks the department has to complete by that fast-approaching deadline. Sometimes our goals put us in direct competition with other parts of the organisation.

How often have you been to a meeting when you have prepared your position beforehand? You feel good about the meeting because you have prepared well. Unfortunately someone you work alongside chooses to take a counter position and she has done her preparation well also. The general manager who is chairing the meeting allows you each to keep debating your positions in an attempt to win over 'the other side'. The meeting overruns, no agreement is reached, and tempers are frayed. The only action agreed is to meet again in a week's time to discuss the topic further.

Finally there is the barrier of behaviour. In our organisation, with many trained engineers and other graduates, the culture was one of not showing signs of weakness by having to ask for help. If someone did ask for help, you were too busy anyway with your own priorities, and your boss would not approve of your helping another department.

I wonder if the people in the meeting above were actively listening to each other's argument to check that they understood it. Did they take the time to acknowledge the point, or were they merely using the time the other was speaking to construct the next point of argument?

We can tackle each of these barriers separately but it is the combination that will ensure the creation of an attractive environment for knowledge sharing.

Within BP we have just moved to the third version of our 'common operating environment' (COE), a standard for computers, software and communications. We have done this across the former BP, Amoco, Arco and Burmah-Castrol companies, reaching some 100,000 people. The cost of doing this was significant ($300 million). What are the benefits to a company like ours?

Connecting the company via a common operating environment

We are all connected. We can share documents and information across the globe quickly by having the same standard software, hardware and naming conventions. We can dock into, and log onto, the company network and access our e-mail, our personal and shared documents from any BP office in the world, from Alaska to Vietnam, from China to Mexico. In addition we can connect in from home, from the airport or from the hotel room. We can stay connected from wherever we are in the world.

We can quickly share documents, store them in a common place, use common search and access methods, and have discussion forums to tap into the diversity of expertise within our organisation. We can jointly collaborate in the construction of a presentation or document without physically being in the same place. Although none of these capabilities are truly 'leading edge', the ability to be able to work in this way across an entire organisation, every day, is extremely powerful. It removes so many of the barriers to sharing.

In order to do this we have to give up some independence. We have similar hardware, the same software and the same version of that software. We do not always move to the latest version. For instance we used Windows 95 as our operating system for five years after it was first released! *Common* is more important to us than *current*. There was a time when one of our business streams had standardised on Apple Macintosh computers. We swapped them for IBM machines, in the interests of sharing with the whole organisation.

> The common operating environment has been a great enabler, but on its own not sufficient to ensure the sharing of know-how. Think about your own organisation. What are the barriers in your organisation to sharing knowledge?

The processes and organisation of BP

A recent question sent by a member of the public to the 'Ask Sir John' spot on BP's Internet site (www.bp.com) was: 'Can you describe how BP uses and values knowledge management techniques?'

His response was:

> *'The effective management of know-how and knowledge is central to both the delivery of today's performance and to the future success of the company. In my view, the key to real success in being a knowledge-based company is in the way we organise ourselves,*

and the behaviours we exhibit. Our experience has shown that an organisation based on a federation of self-standing business units is very good for delivering financial performance, but is not ideal for transferring know-how around the company. For this reason we have created a number of so called peer processes:

Making use of peer processes

- *peer groups share know-how amongst senior group managers at the portfolio and resource allocation level;*

- *peer reviews expose specific business activities to the challenge and scrutiny of senior professionals and leaders from similar business activities around the group; and*

- *peer assists are used at the professional specialist level to make sure the right know-how gets to the right place at the right time.*

'We also encourage all staff to become members of lateral networks across the organisation – where they belong to communities with similar interests. We believe outstanding business performance comes from liberating our staff, creating a culture where they feel comfortable asking for and offering help.'

So BP has put peer processes in place to improve the sharing of know-how between businesses. Not every process encourages sharing of know-how however. One group of businesses were set a target of reducing running costs by 25 per cent with a clear implication that those under-performing would be sold. The businesses had survival on their mind rather than sharing, especially with 'competitors' within the same organisation. Common goals engender a spirit of win-win, that is, everyone can succeed through helping others by sharing what they know.

Back to that meeting that you prepared so well for earlier. A more successful meeting can deliver results by encouraging an atmosphere of sharing experiences and then working together on creating a solution. For more on this process see Chapter 6, Learning From Your Peers, p. 57.

> Whether you are a large or small organisation, have you considered using some peers – inside or outside – to help design your piece of work?

Behaviours

'Help' is a four-letter word! It's a word we all know the meaning of, but are reluctant to utter. We have been educated to solve problems ourselves. If we have not done something before then we are encouraged to figure out how to achieve it. We often consider it a sign of weakness to ask someone else for some help. However, it's amazing how willing people are to give up their time if someone asks for help. The requestor gets lots of support to do a better job than he could have done on his own. At the very least he considers a wider range of opportunities.

Making it easy to ask for help

One colleague of ours, Frank, used this facet of human nature when he wanted to share something he felt was a good practice. He was frustrated that his good ideas had been ignored before. This time he had a great process for prioritising IT services. Instead of making a presentation to 'sell' his idea, he requested help to improve his process. The result? He improved his process still further and three people took his process away to implement in their own offices.

To encourage people to offer their help we advocate rewarding people with the right behaviours. This reward is rarely financial but, instead, acknowledges that their contribution made a difference. Within BP some businesses include a review of sharing know-how as an integral part of their annual appraisal.

Developing relationships

Sharing with someone you know

We share things better with people we know and trust. Would you lend your watch to a total stranger? Now would you lend your watch to your neighbour at work? It's the same with knowledge. Phil, a consultant who routinely works with us, put it this way:

'I wouldn't share a secret with a roomful of people'.

Instead he shares something minor to see if there is the basis for a relationship and then looks for reciprocity and trust to develop.

We are going to need to develop new ways of forming relationships, as we routinely get knowledge from others via the web, or across a large organisation, without meeting face to face. We have not solved that yet, and when time and money permit we meet face-to-face as a precursor to exchanging know-how. Indeed, a key part of the process between the authors and the publishers of this book was to meet and lunch together in order to develop rapport. Many of the subsequent exchanges have been held via phone or e-mail. In the world of e-business we may not be able to meet all of our customers face to face. We will have to find new ways to develop rapport electronically.

> *'"Connectedness and openness" have taken over from "secrecy and empire building" as keys to personal and collective success.'*

Whether with a friend or a stranger, sharing of knowledge is better if people develop active listening skills. What is active listening? Our definition is that people spend time understanding what the person means, and replaying it in **Active listening** their own words to check that understanding as a precursor to stating whether they agree with it and why.

> *'So you mean to say that if I say what I heard back to you, then we'll both have a clearer understanding?'*

That's right! In our experience, too may people queue up to speak rather than listen to what others have to say.

Another behaviour that is key to sharing knowledge is giving and receiving a challenge. Challenging assumptions or someone's firmly-held beliefs takes some effort, as does receiving such a challenge.

In the course of reading this book, you have probably read something that you wish to challenge us on, haven't you? Have a think about how you might do it in a way that would not cause offence or defence.

Leadership

Our experience is that no one likes to be told to change their behaviour by someone clearly not exhibiting that behaviour. ('Do as I say, not as I do ... ') Good leadership is demonstrated by managers who exhibit good active listening, who check their understanding, who ask 'What have you learned from others?' and who acknowledge when they have learned something from you.

Setting the right environment is fundamental to enable sharing to happen naturally. In BP this has been achieved by:

1. Providing a common operating environment to enable the whole organisation to be connected in order to share documents and knowledge.

2. Creating a series of peer processes to enable cross-business sharing.

3. Encouraging the right behaviours; behaviours such as asking for help, active listening, challenging, developing relationships and building trust.

So, now it's time to get started!

GETTING STARTED – JUST DO IT

5

It's one thing understanding what knowledge management is. Understanding that the KM model has several components, each of which adds value, is helpful. Getting the environment right helps. But what then? We could spend a lifetime learning before doing, but unless we get into action we will never achieve anything.

In this chapter:

- Start with 'where the business is'.

- Stop procrastinating and just do something simple.

- Review what you have done and set the next steps.

- A knowledge store doesn't have to be electronic!

How do *you* solve jigsaw puzzles? I usually sort out the four corners and the edge pieces, put them together and then work towards the middle. My sister collects similar colours together. A friend starts with the first pieces he picks up and compares them to the picture. His brother is more extreme, as he puts it together without looking at the picture till he has finished! Usually we each have a preferred strategy to get us started, and we may modify our approach if we are struggling to put it together.

Have you ever sat there and looked at the picture and the pieces until you have figured out how it all goes together? Unlikely. There are just too many parts to hold in your head at once. So it is with knowledge management. We want to learn before doing, but there comes a time when we just have to get started.

Start with where the business is

Understanding the critical business issues is not enough. Studying examples of what others have done is useful. The very next step is to do something, and learn from doing it. Very often when we discussed knowledge management with a business team they would say:

> *'We think this is really good. The only problem is that we don't have the time right now on top of everything else we have to do.'*

Our response to this was:

Having the time to halve the time

> *'What if we told you someone else has already done the very task you are about to do. We just need to find out who and what they learned.'*

We even invented a slogan 'Having the time to halve the time.' In other words if you make time to work on this it will save you a lot of time in the long run.

- In China, BP had entered into a new joint venture to build and operate a chemicals factory. What were the issues that they didn't know they needed to know?

- BP was developing a project in Vietnam to create a gas and power industry, in a country that has little money and a big need for power in order to develop. They had reached a stand-off in commercial negotiations.

> *'We were negotiating 10 independent commercial contracts. We needed assistance in managing information and relationships. Our first goal was to know if we could reach a deal.'*

- In Europe, Bovis were building a large number of petrol filling stations for BP. Could they build them more efficiently?

Do something simple

No amount of theory will actually impact your business results. It's time to stop procrastinating. Get up off your seat and start doing something! Ensure that what you do is simple – no need to create an air of mystique.

In China, the KM team found a simple question to ask, *'What do we need to learn?'* Then they listened to the responses. This was very much about learning before getting into action. This started a conversation with individuals and with small groups, speculating on the future by reflecting on the past.

Start with a question or a review

What do *you* need to learn?

In Vietnam the question posed was *'What is your key issue?'* It was essentially a 'pause for breath', a review of what had, and had not, been achieved. What was interesting was the diversity of responses from the key people in the team. They each saw the issue from a different perspective.

In Europe, after the first petrol filling station had been completed, all those involved met to review the work. They followed the format of an After Action Review, borrowed from the US Army (see Chapter 7, p. 75).

As a principle, if the business teams were already in action, the starting point was an After Action Review, starting with the four standard questions. The event under review might be a meeting, a successful negotiation or an unsuccessful advertising campaign. For example you may have been promoting a project to the board, failing to sell a new product to a customer, or attempting to secure funding for a new venture.

Review what you have done and set the next steps

In China the team listened carefully to all the questions. That night in the hotel room they summarised what they had heard and the differences between the responses. They designed some new questions based on the responses. 'What do you need to know next?'

In Vietnam, after three days of interviewing and refining the questions, the team felt that they had a good grasp of the key issues. They reviewed what they had learned with the management team, who were amazed by how much the questioning had revealed. It provoked further conversation between the management team, in which tacit knowledge flowed. For example, one of the key negotiators shared how he prepared for the forthcoming negotiation. The strong body language indicated that it was knowledge that he had obviously not thought to share with his peers before.

In Europe the team made changes to their processes and procedures and built the next station, faster and cheaper. They met again the next day to carry out the After Action Review, keen to improve further.

What then?

Let's look at how a practical, stepwise programme was implemented in Vietnam, as an example.

The business appointed a knowledge manager to initiate and co-ordinate the whole process. Here's what he had to say:

> 'You need a dedicated resource. People don't do this stuff in their spare time. You need a central person, and also you need a person in each team who has bought in to the process, otherwise it won't work. Choose someone who talks a lot! A KM person has to be a communicator, has to get out there, find information, and feed it back again. Establishing me as knowledge manager meant that I was the focal point for anyone.

A good communicator

I could respond to gossip by offering knowledge in return; "Did you know this?" It became two-way.

'We used AARs extensively. Each team had a 15-minute debrief using the AAR format, after each discussion with the government. This was a very powerful tool within the team. They could look back at what they did, and change what they doing the next day.

A weekly summary

'The AAR proformas had a distribution list, and I produced a weekly consolidation and also lessons learnt, and put it out to everyone. The weekly summary was good; if people had no time to read the AARs I would summarise each one into 2 or 3 sentences and highlight the key stuff.

'The meetings tended to be in Hanoi. People passed through the office on their way to and from the meeting. The "war room" had to be physical. The charts we made of the deal process, and of the structure of the Vietnam government organisation were too big to go on a PC, so we had them on the wall with a pen at the side. People could contribute by using the pen; they did not have to log on. When we had a discussion we could go in the room, update the charts rapidly, share it easily.'

A knowledge store ('war room')

Bruce MacFarlane

The key was keeping the system simple, concise and effective. Reviews took 15 minutes, weekly notes were 1 or 2 pages, the chart was simple, and the software was simple. Because the community of practice was entirely local, the knowledge was stored in a physical room and it encouraged interaction. The information was useful and accessible so people started going in there before the meetings too ...

So in summary:

- Don't procrastinate. Get started right away!

- Start with where the business is, review where they are compared to where they were meant to be and determine what you can learn from that.

- Do something simple.

- Review and plan the next steps.

- Go and look at your knowledge management model to determine where you can next make a difference.

The next six chapters offer you some tools and techniques to help make that difference. If you like what you've heard so far, then you'll know what you are looking for. What will it feel like when you have achieved what you are striving for?

- For learning before, look at Chapter 6 (p. 57).

- For learning whilst doing, go to Chapter 7 (p. 75), to give you time to reflect.

- Read Chapter 8 (p. 87), if you want to learn after doing.

- If you want to know *who* to talk to try Chapter 9 (p. 103), or Chapter 10 (p. 123) if it's developing a sense of community that you are looking for.

- Chapter 11 (p. 141) will give you some insights into capturing knowledge.

Part

Tools and Techniques

2

LEARNING FROM YOUR PEERS
– SOMEBODY HAS ALREADY DONE IT

In this chapter we discuss:

- Setting up a meeting to learn from others.

- Why do it and when?

- Steps involved in a peer assist meeting.

- Who do you invite?

- Some examples of peer assist in use.

It was just after Christmas and I was getting round to thinking about my holidays for the coming year, when Clive came for dinner. He brought with him some photos of a walking holiday in the Pyrenees. He had obviously enjoyed it and went through in great detail how the holiday company transported his luggage, how he had met up with the same people each breakfast and evening for a meal, and how the hotels were warm and friendly. During the day he was alone on the hills with a friend, but walking a given route so people knew where he was.

I explained what our situation was, that the children were going to 'do their own thing', and that for the first time my wife and I could choose to do what we wanted. Clive sent us the holiday brochure he had used and explained the ranking system for difficulty of walk. We also talked with a friend who had done a walking holiday and learned what she had found useful and what she would avoid another time. I sat down with my wife and we analysed what we had heard and what we thought was right for us. We selected a two-boot (moderately energetic!) holiday in the Jura region of France in May. We shared what we had chosen with Clive and our friend. They were pleased we had used their advice.

We thoroughly enjoyed our holiday. Without Clive's visit we may have spent it on a conventional package tour to Greece. We adapted what we had learned to ensure that we had a holiday that was right for us and different from normal.

What is a peer assist?

Sharing experience, insights and knowledge

Stated simply a peer assist is a meeting or workshop where people are invited from other teams to share their experience, insights and knowledge with a team who have requested some help. A peer assist is all about a team asking for help, and it is for their benefit. Somewhere within BP, a peer assist is happening every week.

A peer assist:

- targets a specific technical or commercial challenge;

- gains assistance and insight from people outside the team;

- identifies possible approaches and new lines of inquiry;

- promotes sharing of learning with each other; and

- develops strong networks amongst staff.

Why do it and when?

It's worth holding a peer assist when a business unit is facing a challenge, where the knowledge and experience of others will really help, and when the potential business benefits outweigh the cost of travel.

Here are some quotes from businesses that have used the process:

> 'I have just finished a peer assist where we saved the site something like $12–20 million and the company a number we are still trying to calculate.'

> 'A retail lubricants peer assist in South Africa saved £15 million in two days.'

> 'The power of the peer assist was not that it told us something we didn't know but rather that it got us into action to prevent us going down the same path as others.'

What is involved in a peer assist?

The concept of peer assist is quite simple and it is more than just sharing good practice. Experience and knowledge is gained in a particular situation or context. Knowledge is therefore context-dependent and doesn't always transfer easily to a different context.

Let's look at a 2 by 2 matrix. We cannot go far wrong in a management book presenting a 2 by 2 matrix can we?!

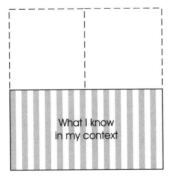

What I know
in my context

Having requested a peer assist, I share what I know based on the context in which I learned it.

You then share what you know based on your context.

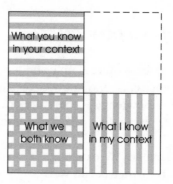

Together we learn what we both know and what we can learn from each other.

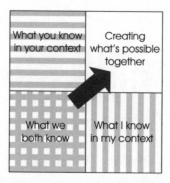

We are then in a position to work together to determine what is possible, either by adapting the practice to work in the new context or by creating something new from what we both know.

And from those possibilities we can take some action.

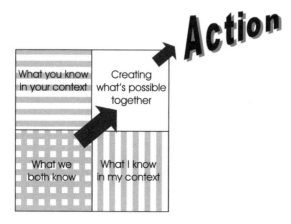

That is the essence of the peer assist process.

12 steps to plan a peer assist

Several people have asked us how to go about planning a peer assist. There is no single right way to hold a peer assist, but here is a method that has worked well inside BP. Inside BP, peer assists are held between professionals with a wealth of international experience. Decide if it works for you. Here's a starting point – digest and adapt it.

There are 12 steps:

1. Clarify the purpose.

2. Check whether someone has already solved the problem.

3. Identify a facilitator.

4. Consider the timing and schedule a date.

5. Select a diverse group of participants.

6. Get clear on the desired deliverables and how you might achieve them.

7. Plan time for socialising.

8. Spend some time setting the environment.

9. Divide the time available into four parts, start with sharing information and context.

10. Encourage the visitors to ask what they need to know.

11. Analyse what you have heard.

12. Present the feedback, consider what each has learned, and who else might benefit. Agree actions and report progress.

Let's go through these steps in more detail.

1. Communicate a clear purpose

Peer assists work well when the purpose is clear and you communicate that purpose to participants.

Define the specific problem you are trying to get help with, consider whether a peer assist is the most appropriate process, then write a terms of reference.

Facilitator's notes:
If you are the facilitator, get clear on the purpose of the peer assist and be sure that the person holding it genuinely wants to learn something. Ideally they are targeting the peer assist to address one of the key business risks. If the stated purpose is to gain endorsement or to get others to use 'my' method, then advise them that they require some other sort of meeting.

2. Has the problem already been solved?

Consider whether someone else has already solved the problem. Have a look at the company knowledge base to find out what others have already learned. Share your peer assist plans with others. They may have similar needs.

For example, several refineries held peer assists to improve cost savings. This involved some people repeating the exercise at many refineries in different parts of the world. A more efficient way might have been to hold a peer assist at a single refinery and extract the common lessons for all refineries to adopt.

3. Get a facilitator

Identify a facilitator for the meeting who is external to the team. The role of the facilitator is to ensure that by managing the process the meeting participants reach the desired outcome. The facilitator may or may not record the event; make sure you agree roles beforehand. Plan the details of the peer assist in conjunction with the facilitator. Clarify the purpose and the desired outcome, and then plan the time to achieve that.

4. Timing is important

Schedule a date for the peer assist. Ensure it is early enough to do something different with what you have learned. Plan the peer assist early to make use of the help to deliver your business outcome. People frequently hold them too close to the decision date to make a real impact. Ask yourself 'If I get a result we do not expect, will I have time to do anything about it?' Give yourself time to apply the knowledge and be prepared for the unexpected. After all you didn't invite people just to endorse your ideas. Did you?

Will I have time to do something different?

Consider the timing, who is available on your selected dates, when are the holidays?

How long does a peer assist last? This depends on the complexity of the problem and the familiarity of the team with the context. Our experience has been that the majority of peer assists are one-and-a-half to two days long, although something useful can be exchanged in half a day.

5.   Select the participants

Once the purpose is clear, develop a list of potential participants who have the diversity of skills, competencies and experience needed for the peer assist. Six to eight people is ideal. Sometimes we observe that the same people turn up again and again. Avoid the 'usual suspects' and bring some fresh ideas into the discussion. Go to Chapter 9, p. 103 for further insights on picking the right help.

Go for diversity and avoid the 'usual suspects'

Facilitator's notes:
Watch for the balance between the visitors and the home team. Avoid the urge to invite the whole project team into the meeting. It's easy to overwhelm the visitors and stifle new thinking.

6.   Get clear about the deliverables

Get clear on the desired deliverables of the peer assist, and then plan the time to achieve that. Prepare carefully; optimise the time spent together, and make use of the knowledge gained. The deliverables should comprise options and insights rather than the answer. It is up to the person who asked for the assistance to decide upon the actions.

Provide the participants with any briefing materials early enough for them to review them prior to the actual peer assist.

Be clear in articulating both the objective of the peer assist and the business problem or challenge for which you are asking the group to provide input. Be prepared for these to be 'reframed' in the course of the challenge.

Get to the root cause

What do we mean by reframe the challenge? The problem you have identified might well be the symptom rather than the root cause. Let me give you an example.

I attended a peer assist where the business manager was looking for some insights and options to make his gas project a more attractive investment. In setting the context, the focus was on the months of work that his engineering team had undertaken to take out unnecessary costs. This included investigating imaginative ways to use less materials, to reduce the construction cost, and to defer costs until some gas, and hence money, was flowing.

What might they have forgotten? Would the combined brainpower of their peers come up with a solution based on their own experiences of large projects?

After checking they understood the issues, the peers started talking about their own experiences. Viewing the problem for the first time, they rapidly came up with a number of alternatives. One option provided the breakthrough.

The focus of the business team had been on reducing costs. They wanted a better return on investment before they committed to spend the large amounts of money required. What if they focused instead on getting a better return? Returns on investment *Be prepared to* were constrained by the terms of the contract with the *see the world* government in which they were working, as the business *through fresh* manager had been told by the government not to discuss *eyes* re-negotiation. The experience of peers was that it was better to talk to the government early, discuss the problem and look for ways that both the company and the government could meet their objectives. After all, the country needed the money from royalties every bit as much as BP needed an acceptable return on investment.

The next day the business manager called his contact in the government to arrange a meeting. Thereafter the balance of activity shifted from engineering to contract negotiations.

Fresh eyes often see the world through different lenses and help you focus on the root cause.

Now you have completed the planning, you're about 60% of the way there. Well done! Grab yourself a coffee, go back to your desk and put your feet up for five minutes!

7.   Ensure that the team socialise

Allow time in the agenda for the team to get to know one another. The team needs to socialise; this may be a dinner the night before, or half an hour over coffee at the start of the day; something to start building rapport. Remember, this is a temporary but newly-formed team. For the group to work openly together, to make and receive challenge, to have pet projects put under the microscope, it is important that people get to know each other. If you cannot manage this, plan dinner for the evening between the two days. It is amazing how much knowledge is transferred over a glass of wine and a good meal! One team started by sharing a communal Japanese bath together. But this is not absolutely essential to ensure a successful peer assist!

8.   Define the purpose and lay the ground rules

So that's all the preparation, what about the meeting itself?

Spend some time setting the environment and stating expected behaviours. If it's useful, use the matrix diagram to explain the sharing of knowledge.

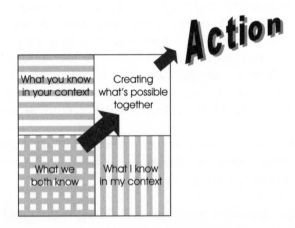

Brief the host team to listen in order to understand and to seek opportunities. A defensive reaction will deter the visitors from offering their insights.

Design the day ensuring plenty of opportunity to reflect. We achieve this by asking a few simple questions.

The role of the peer assist participants is to offer help, know-how and experience to resolve the challenge without adding to the workload. However, some contention will raise the level of discussion. This will not occur if the group is being too polite.

Facilitator notes:
Ensure that the contention is focused on the activity rather than the person.

Participants should recommend what the host team should stop doing as well as what extra they might do. Their time is limited, it's about prioritising and focusing their effort onto the things that will make a difference.

9.   Start by sharing information and context

Most of the peer assists we have been involved with last for one-and-a-half to two days. Divide the meeting time into four roughly equal parts. Clearly articulate the purpose of bringing the peer-assist team together and make a clear request of the team. During the first quarter, get the resident team to present the context, the history and the plans for the future. Resist the temptation of having too many from the home team, and *telling* too much. You want only to say enough to get the peer-assist team started in the right direction. They can ask questions if they want to know more.

Ensure that the visitors have sufficient time to contribute

The visitors have travelled and have given up some of their precious time to help you. Listen to what they have to say. There was one peer assist in London to which an engineer from Trinidad had been invited. He had travelled overnight for ten hours to help, but despite efforts to involve him, he wasn't given the space to say what he thought of their plans.

Facilitator's notes:
Keep context presentations short and sharp. There is a strong tendency for any information presented becoming the focus of discussion. Avoid this by finding out what the visitors want to know.

10.   Encourage the visitors to ask questions and give feedback

In the second part the visitors take up the baton. They consider what they have heard and discuss 'what they have learned that has surprised them' and 'what they haven't heard that they expected to.' The home team should take a back seat at this stage and maybe even exit the room. The peer-assist team then decide their course of action. What else do they need to know and whom do they know who knows? It may be that they want to talk to others to get their viewpoints at this stage, to talk to operational people or experts, customers or government officials. Set up some interviews, or make telephone or videoconference calls. Get views from contractors, external bodies or local staff if relevant. Request data and reports. What do they need to know to address the problem at hand? Remember it's not the job of the peer-assist team to solve it but to offer some options and insights based on their unique experiences.

Facilitator's notes:
Feedback is an essential part of the learning process. Allow time at the end of each day for feedback. Use an After Action Review (see Chapter 7, Learning Whilst Doing, p. 75) if appropriate, to help set the direction for the following day.

11. Analyse what you have heard

The third part of the meeting is for analysing and reflecting on what you have learned. By all means involve a couple of the home team but make sure they don't close off options too quickly or drive towards their preferred outcome. They should be there to listen and learn. At this stage you are examining options.

Towards the end of this phase create a presentation to give to the wider home team. What have you learned, what options do you see and what has worked elsewhere? Tell the story of how it has worked elsewhere rather than 'you ought to…'

We find storyboarding a useful technique here (see Appendix A, p. 199).

12. Present the feedback and agree on actions

The last step for the visitors is to present their feedback to the team and to answer questions. Avoid getting into debate at this stage. As in all feedback, start with what has been done well and then what options there are to do things differently. Focus on the activity rather than the people. Finish with a general positive statement. On the receiving end, don't expect a silver bullet, a single solution to all of your challenges, a sudden flash of inspiration that tells you your problems are solved. Frequently the home team feel nothing new has come up. Remember the visitors are reflecting what they have been told, coupled with what they know

Don't expect a silver bullet

in their context. Often they confirm what you are doing is right but may set your priorities somewhat differently. The peer assist may increase your confidence to do something that is a difficult decision to take.

The person who set up the peer assist should acknowledge the help and the time people have given up. He or she should also commit to when (s)he will get back with an action list of what the team are going to do differently. (S)he may decide to invite the peer assist team back for future help. The benefit of this would be that they would not need to learn the context again and the peers can gain satisfaction from remaining connected with the project.

Next have the visitors reflect for five minutes then say what *they* have learned that they will take away and apply. Learning is never one-way, although the peer assist may start out along those lines. Offer what you learn to others, and provide a contact name for follow-up discussions.

Learning is never one way

Consider who else might benefit from the lessons learned and the best way of doing that. Share the lessons learned with these individuals. Provide contact names for follow up discussions and progress reports. Reusing knowledge is a smart way to avoid duplicate effort. For tips on capturing what you have learned go to Chapter 11, Leveraging What We've Learned – Capturing Knowledge, p. 141.

Consider who else might benefit from the lessons

Finally carry out an After Action Review (see Chapter 7). Did the peer assist go according to plan? What was different and why was there a difference? And what can you learn from that?

> Stop and consider for a moment. Could you apply this process to a piece of work that you have just started, or plan to start shortly? Why not use the 12 steps in the resources section to plan your own peer assist?

Who are the right people to invite to a peer assist?

Sir John Browne, the chief executive of BP, observed in a recent interview for *HBR* that:

'The politics accompanying hierarchies hamper the free exchange of knowledge. People are much more open with their peers. They are much more willing to share and to listen.'

Look across the hierarchy not up it. Make sure the participants are peers – peers can be more open, and challenge without being threatening. Ask the discipline head to suggest some names, so he or she is assured that the right challenge will be offered, but do not invite the discipline head to attend.

Look across the hierarchy

It's often the same people who turn up to help ('the usual suspects'). The risk with this is that no fresh ideas are circulated, and only the usual suspects become knowledgeable. Assemble a group of participants that have diverse skills and experience. Include people who will both challenge your mental models and offer options and new lines of inquiry. Let others decide whether they have something to contribute, rather than picking them. Consider including people from other disciplines, businesses, and companies. When partners and external folks are involved this adds to the value of the assist. Why? The more experience from different contexts that you can access, the greater the number of dimensions with which to illuminate your problem. Small teams or syndicates (six to eight people) are more effective for working options.

But where will you find them if they are not to be the usual suspects?

At the simplest level it can be people working on different projects farther down your corridor. In a larger company, use a company Yellow Pages on the intranet. (See Chapter 9, Finding the Right People, p. 103.) Or look elsewhere on the intranet for someone with the skills and experience to help you. If you don't have a knowledge directory or intranet then ask the head of the discipline or function to suggest some names.

Secondly, make use of any functional networks. These have the knowledge to suggest who might bring something to your business or technical issue. It is, incidentally, a good way for individuals and teams to 'view and be viewed without obligation' in case there is a vacancy in the future.

Consider posting an announcement of your peer assist well ahead of time. It will be worth looking to see if someone is already planning one on a similar topic. Perhaps you can join forces and help each other.

One idea tried by a business in Norway was to invite a team who was further along in its project to review its work. In this case, it is often worth inviting the entire team to do the peer assist, rather than putting together a set of individuals. This has the following advantages:

- the team dynamics are already in place, and the peer assist is therefore more effective;

- the disciplines are covered, and there should be no gaps;

- the cross-discipline awareness is already in place; and

- there is an increased empathy with the host team, about to experience problems the visiting team has already solved.

If you are working with a smaller organisation, consider getting help externally. We have found that people love to help, and that they always learn something for themselves as a consequence. Generally, they are flattered to be asked.

OK, so now I know what a peer assist is, why and when to do it, what the steps are and whom I should invite? Let me give you some examples.

What topics?

Our first experience of a really good peer assist was a relatively low-key meeting called by a geologist before he wrote his project plan. As Steve observed, 'It's a common mistake for people to think, "We won't call them in until we have something concrete to show them; lets draw up our plans and bring people in to endorse them."' He invited people who were working on, or had completed, other projects in different parts of the world in a similar geological setting. *Developing the project plan* He asked each of them to tell their story of how they had gone about their project. He asked them what had gone well, and what they would do differently if they did it over again. The group listed what was important in starting the geologist's project, given the different contextual setting. A facilitator captured the list of whats, whys and hows on a flip chart. This formed the basis for developing the project plan.

Another was to learn how to improve negotiations with a variety of Government agencies. One clear message that came out, was to put more effort into building relationships relative to the effort put into the technical understanding. Martin said 'The fundamental lesson we drew from the experience is that we spend too much early effort on tasks trying to solve the technical and commercial problems and not enough time on the softer issues like getting to know our partners.'

Building relationships

Here's another example. The context was that the project engineering team was about to spend a lot on some engineering design work before committing to construct the surface facilities to produce gas in the Sahara desert. The project team wanted to gain assurance that their plans were sound and that they had identified the key business and technical drivers to maximise the value of the project.

A collection of peers arrived from Aberdeen, Vietnam, Wytch Farm oilfield in S. England and Trinidad. They were people running projects in different geographical locations, and at different stages of operation. They met with representatives from the project team the night before to have dinner together and to set the context and agree the purpose of the peer assist. As a result of this session the peer assist was reframed from, 'are we doing the project right?' to 'are we doing the right project given the business and political context?' and, 'is the pace right?'

Is it the right project?

The peers offered the following insights:

- They supported the engineering design work proposed since this clarified whether it was worth proceeding.

- They felt it was important to keep progress on the engineering project in step with all other parts, such as marketing.

- They had major concerns about aligning our needs with those of the National Oil company, our partners in the project.

- They thought that the project team needed to clarify the prerequisites for making a positive decision to go ahead with construction.

- They pointed out that the strategy needed reviewing following the merger of BP with Amoco. The increased portfolio alters both our capital exposure and the impact on the country.

The project team agreed a number of actions, which they copied to the peers within two weeks of the meeting and subsequently provided them with an update on progress. The business unit leader and the project manager took up the strategic issues.

This peer assist tackled the broader issues of identifying and shaping the right project as well as whether the project team were going about the project in the right way. For them, shaping the project to make the right investment was the foundation for assuring the project was being tackled correctly.

Agree actions and report on progress

These three examples should give you an idea of the range of topics that we have discussed at a peer assist.

Have a think about where you might apply a peer assist. You may consider trying the process to tackle a bullying problem in a local school, or to develop ideas for fund-raising activities for your favourite charity. You don't have to limit yourself to workplace situations.

Summary

Finally, here's a summary of what we have learned about peer assists over the last few years.

- Peer assists work well when the purpose is clear and you communicate that purpose to participants. Be prepared for the purpose to be reframed during the course of the meeting.

- Consider whether someone else has already solved the problem in which case you don't need to meet. Share your peer-assist plans with others. They may have similar needs.

- Ensure the peer assist is early enough to do something different with what you have learned. Ask yourself 'If I get a result we do not expect, will I have time to do anything about it?'

- Invite potential participants who have the diversity of skills, competencies and experience needed for the peer assist. Include people who will both challenge your mental models and offer options and new lines of inquiry.

- Listen for understanding and how you might improve your activity. Defending the status quo will not improve your project.

- The role of the peer-assist participants is to offer help, know-how and experience to resolve the challenge without adding to the workload. Get participants to recommend what the host team should stop doing as well as what extra they might do.

- At the end have each participant consider what they have learned and will apply from the peer assist. And ask them to consider who else might benefit from your learning.

- Finally, ask the host team to share progress against an action list with the participants of the peer assist, as their project develops.

That completes the chapter on 'Learning before doing'. What other learning tools would you like to know about? The following two chapters cover 'Learning whilst doing' and 'Learning after doing'.

LEARNING WHILST DOING
– TIME TO REFLECT

In this chapter:

- Why learning whilst doing is at the heart of a knowledge culture.

- How to introduce a period of reflection and learning.

- Who should participate.

Lessons from Lara Croft

Have you ever watched a child playing a video game and marveled at how fast they learn?

I find myself doing exactly that with my nine-year-old nephew, Simon. I watch transfixed as he weaves an impossible path through a jungle or labyrinth, cheating death by stopping exactly at the edge of each precipice, knowing exactly how far, when to jump, what to jump on and where all the bonus energy jewels and poison potions lie.

Perhaps this is all easier that it looks. *'Your turn uncle Chris!'*

There goes my reputation for being the cool uncle – seventeen seconds of running, some of it backwards, and then straight down over the edge of the first canyon.

*How children
learn
continuously*
So how do they do it? I spend a fair proportion of my life working at a computer – I was doing it before Simon was born; yet I'm the one who appears totally inept with JungleRaider III, or whatever it was...

It wasn't until I watched Simon tackle level seventy-eight (it was a long game!) – the one that he'd never tackled before, that things became clearer.

'That wasn't supposed to happen.'; 'What if I try this?'; 'There was a jewel here in the last level.'; 'Supposing I jump up here – oops. OK, up there then. Yeesssss!'

Once he was in new territory, he switched from remembering the right sequence, to learning. Continuously learning, doing, testing, checking, learning some more, until he cracked the challenge, and then onto the next level.

That's the behaviour that is so often missing in business. People are happy enough to remember the right sequence – to know the rules of the game. People are happy to work on an important project, and not 'come up for air' until the project close-out. Sometimes, they need to be able to learn quickly, and adapt in order to improve. It's not good

*The challenge
for business
world*
enough to wait for the end of the project for the review to draw out the lessons learned, something needs to change *now*. Wouldn't it be great if that sort of learning was routine in your organisation?

For many years, the US Army has been applying a short, sharp process known as an 'After Action Review' (AAR) to improve their ability to learn in the midst of action and improve teamworking. One of the main drivers for this was their experiences in the Vietnam conflict.

At the peak of the conflict, it became apparent that foot soldiers in the field had far more knowledge about what was going on than head-

*Learning from
the US Army
– the After
Action Review*
quarters. AARs were introduced to pass timely, relevant learning within and between teams of soldiers at times when waiting for a full evaluation report would mean waiting too long. To quote from the US Army handbook: *A Leader's Guide to After Action Reviews*, which is readily accessible on the Internet:

An After Action Review (AAR) is a professional discussion of an event, focused on performance standards, that enables soldiers to discover for themselves what happened, why it happened, and how to sustain strengths and improve on weaknesses. It is a tool leaders and units can use to get maximum benefit from every mission or task. It provides:

- *candid insights into specific soldier, leader, and unit strengths and weaknesses from various perspectives;*

- *feedback and insight critical to battle-focused training; and*

- *details often lacking in evaluation reports alone.*

When do you hold an AAR?

A common misconception regarding AARs is that they should only be carried out at the end of a formal project or sizeable piece of work. This is not the case. AARs are actually designed to aid team and individual learning *during* the work process and can be conducted after any identifiable event. An event can be either an entire small action or a discrete part of a larger action, e.g. a shift handover or a project planning meeting.

Using AARs during the work process, not after it

Perhaps you have recently commissioned some market research, or secured an important contract?

Perhaps you have just completed a series of interviews for a new recruit?

Events suitable for AARs simply have a beginning and an end, an identifiable purpose and some metrics on which performance can be measured (for learning after the project is complete, see the chapter on 'learning after doing').

How do AARs work?

AARs are a simple way for individuals and teams to learn *immediately*, from both successes and failures, regardless of the length of the task in question. The learning is by the team, for the team. The format is very simple and quick – it's a 'pencil and paper' or flipchart exercise. In an open and honest meeting, usually no longer than twenty minutes, each participant in the event answers four simple questions:

Four simple questions

- What was supposed to happen?

- What actually happened?

- Why were there differences?

- What did we learn?

Team learning, and building trust, and team integrity are equal objectives of the process. Our experience was that the simplicity of the process and the low time requirements were key to its acceptance. To quote from a supervisor at Toledo Refinery in Ohio:

> *'There are times when you think "we don't have time to do this", then you do it and you think, "we don't have time not to do this."'*

What a fantastic quote! We often struggle to break into peoples' routines when we introduce new initiatives, processes and ways of working because the burden is simply too great.

Let's try something before we go any further in this chapter.

Take a few minutes and reflect on something that you did yesterday.

Can you imagine it? Can you remember what was said? How did you feel?

Now answer the four AAR questions:

- What was supposed to happen?

- What actually happened?

- Why were there differences?

- What can you learn from this?

What does that tell you about what you could do differently tomorrow?

That is what you can get from a small amount of personal reflection. Just imagine what a team could achieve by taking time out to reflect similarly on what they have achieved.

AARs are simple to remember and simple to use. Because of this ease of use, they became quickly adopted and implemented by operations staff at several different parts of our business. We use the following guidelines when introducing AARs to BP.

1. Hold the AAR immediately

AARs are carried out immediately whilst all of the participants are still available, and their memories are fresh. Learning can then be applied right away, even on the next day.

In BP Vietnam, AARs were held immediately after every meeting with the Vietnamese authorities, as a means of building up a knowledge of the negotiation process.

> *Reflect on what happened whilst the memory are fresh*

'*Each team had a fifteen minute debrief using the AAR format, after each discussion with the government. This was a very powerful tool within the team. They could look back at what they did, and change what they would do the next day.*'

Bruce MacFarlane

Plan the AAR to fall within the allotted time for the event, so it doesn't appear as an add-on. Include it in the agenda of a meeting, rather than introducing it as an afterthought.

2.   Create the right climate

The ideal climate for an AAR to be successful is one of openness and commitment to learning. AARs are learning events rather than critiques. They certainly should not be treated as personal performance evaluation.

> *'Pin your stripes to the door'*

There can only be one poor performer in an AAR: the one who is not candid about both things that went well and things that did not.

Everyone in the event participates, and everyone is on equal footing. The US Army describe a notion of 'pinning your stripes to the door' – and within the construct of the AAR process, junior soldiers feel completely free to comment on and challenge the actions and instructions of senior staff.

This openness is seen as a vital part of the process of building team integrity. For this team integrity to flourish, there should no spectators, no management oversight – just participants who have earned their right to comment by being part of the action.

3.   Appoint a facilitator

The facilitator of an AAR is not there to 'have' answers, but to help the team to 'learn' answers. People must be drawn out, both for their own learning and the group's learning. What you are trying to get to, is what the Army call 'ground truth' and a facilitator should be able to guide the team to this point – navigating towards some of the unspoken issues.

Sometimes however a facilitator is needed to set the climate of the meeting. The facilitator ensures the meeting is open and that blame is not brought in. He/she must also make sure the process is quick and simple, and owned by the participants. One of the key success factors in an AAR is that everyone has a chance to speak.

Facilitation is an important role for drawing out the learning

The following quote illustrates the power of this factor when working with a multicultural team:

> *'Generally the British are the only ones to speak, so facilitation of the AAR is crucial. I made them answer the AAR questions round the table. You have to try and make the team leader shut up! I got a Vietnamese or a Norwegian to answer the questions first. Obviously I couldn't facilitate all of the meetings, so I excused myself from the process. I said 'AARs are for the people in the team, I am here to facilitate the conversation'. I turned up to the AAR, and made sure the person leading the AAR was not the team leader. Then I pushed my chair as far back as I could, but ensured everyone had their say.'*
>
> Bruce MacFarlane

4..What was supposed to happen?

AARs are very straightforward. The facilitator starts by dividing the event into discrete activities, each of which had (or should have had) an identifiable objective and plan of action. The discussion begins with the first activity: 'what was supposed to happen?' An important discussion follows until all have shared their understanding of what was actually supposed to happen. This is often the most revealing part of the process. Unless there was a clear, well-communicated and unambiguous objective and plan, then it is likely that different members of the team have different understandings of what was supposed to happen. In this event, a successful outcome is unlikely.

Facilitator's notes:
Try asking people to quickly write down their own personal understanding of what was supposed to happen on a scrap of paper. After a couple of minutes ask them to read it back to the group.

The question 'what was supposed to happen?' should be equivalent to 'what were the objectives of the activity?' For example, when reviewing a team meeting, 'what was supposed to happen?' may be better treated as 'to decide, and gain team buy-in to the 2001 strategy', than dwelling on details such as 'we were supposed to start at 8.30, take a 15 minute break for coffee' etc.

Understand the facts – not the opinions – about what really happened

5.   What actually happened?

This means the team must understand facts about what happened – the US Army refer to this as 'ground truth'. Remember, though, that 'ground truth' is there to identify a problem not a culprit.

Facilitator's notes:
This part of the process is vital and can be contentious at times, as people move from theory into reality – don't rush it. Sometimes people will dwell on the mundane aspects of an event when there may be a deeper underlying issue that they find difficult to talk about as a team. If you can encourage one person to make a more personal disclosure about how they felt rather than simply what happened, it can have the effect of 'unblocking' the process, allowing more open exchange to occur.

6.   Now compare the plan with reality

The real learning begins as the team compares the plan to what actually happened in reality and determines, 'why were there differences?' and 'what did we learn?' Successes and shortfalls are identified and discussed. Action plans are then put in place to sustain the successes and to improve upon the shortfalls.

Set in place some actions to embed what has been learned

Facilitator's notes:
Try asking people to quickly write down one key learning for themselves to take away from the meeting. Often the act of writing it down will help the participants to focus on what's important

and memorise the learning for future events. It may be necessary to question quite deeply during this section, repeating the question 'why was this?' in order to get to the underlying reasons.

7.   Recording an AAR

Recording the key elements of an AAR clarifies what happened and compares it to what was supposed to happen.

AARs generate summaries of learning points, which can have high value for the team. That value is often specific to the team in the particular context of the event being reviewed, hence in our experience, AARs are not shared widely – they are primarily *learnings for the team*.

It is useful to capture a record of the AAR points and agreed actions to remind the team of the lessons that were identified. A typical example of this is a two-day meeting or workshop. At the close of day one, a participant conducts a fifteen-minute AAR on the outcomes of that day, and the learning points are captured on a flip chart. At the start of the second day, this flip chart is referred to by the team as a reminder, enabling them to build the lessons of the previous day into their current activity.

Facilitator's notes:
The reality is that in most organisations there is a reluctance to share lessons beyond the immediate team, but there is a willingness to share the corrective actions taken. The key learning points from an AAR are valuable because they are timely – they represent things as they are today, rather than as the product of an audit report. For this reason, it is always worth asking the question: 'is there anyone else with whom we could share what we've learned.'

Power comes from simplicity

In introducing AARs to parts of BP, people were repeatedly struck by the simplicity of the four questions, and the fact that the US Army had institutionalised the process so effectively. One memorable photograph showed soldiers conducting an AAR (complete with flip charts!) in the jungle after a day's action. What possible excuse could a refinery operator, or a team leader have for not creating the space for

> *AARs any time, any place, anywhere ...*

an AAR? Mitch Bowman from Toledo, Ohio is one such leader who rapidly saw the relevance of AARs to his refinery operations:

> *'This process saves a lot of money, big money. A lot of times guys see problems coming before the supervisors. And many won't say anything because it's not their job and no one asks. So the problems happen – there is downtime, big losses. The AAR lets those things come out, ahead of time, just because you're asking.'*
>
> Mitch Bowman

'Just because you're asking' – that is the key point. AARs create the space – just fifteen minutes of it – to ask the key questions

One of the most powerful examples of After Action Reviews having an impact was in the construction of over one hundred retail sites – petrol filling stations – across Europe in 1997. BP worked with its

The benefits – faster delivery and reduced costs

contracting partner Bovis on this major project, and Bovis applied the AAR process after each activity. For example, pouring in the concrete foundations or setting up the pumps. These AARs captured timely lessons that could be applied immediately to the next retail site. By the time the construction programme was completed, Bovis acknowledged that learning tools like AARs had helped to reduce service station build time by two weeks and reduce the cost by 5 per cent.

To make the Army's learning philosophy more tangible, we enlisted the help of retired US Army Colonel, Ed Guthrie. There are times when the tacit knowledge bound up in a practitioner is far more valuable than any number of written facilitator's guides, so we tracked down the 'real McCoy'.

Colonel Ed flew with us to several BP sites around the world and captured the imagination of even the most sceptical of engineers with his colourful war stories.

AARs as personal learning tools

What struck home most to Keith, a member of the team who accompanied Ed to Scotland, was the sense of incompleteness that Ed felt if he hadn't conducted a personal AAR on his day's activities. Before the plane had left Edinburgh airport, Ed already had already produced a scrap of paper and started to ask those four important questions.

Although we haven't embedded After Action Reviews to the same extent as the army, they are widely used across BP's activities. Whether a refinery operations team, an internal workshop, or a meeting with contractors – every day, somewhere in the company those four questions are being asked.

- What was supposed to happen?

- What actually happened?

- Why was there a difference?

- What have we learned?

Of all the learning tools mentioned in this book, in our experience AARs are the easiest ones to introduce. Because of this, they are a great place to start (see Chapter 5, Getting Started – Just Do It, p. 49), if you're looking for an entry point to introduce knowledge management to your organisation.

So what about a tool to help reflection after a larger piece of work or a substantial project? Turn to the next chapter, Learning After Doing – When It's All Over, to learn more about the retrospect process.

LEARNING AFTER DOING
– WHEN IT'S ALL OVER

At the close of a project or any substantial piece of work, it's worth taking a little time to reflect on what has happened, and to capture that for future use of others.

In this chapter we cover:

- A simple process for capturing and transferring lessons from any project or event.

- Detailed guidelines and tips for conducting a review.

- A method for getting to the 'ground truth'.

- Who should participate.

Have you ever wondered what it must be like to be a professional footballer immediately after a defeat? We see the deflated team trail dejectedly from the pitch … but what happens next?

Learning from the football field

At primary school, the dressing rooms could be charged with stinging recriminations, egos were punctured as last week's hero became this week's villain.

'Six–five! Collison, you cost us the game – why didn't you pass the ball?'

(Thinks) *'Six–five. Why* didn't *I pass the ball?'*

In professional circles, of course, things are somewhat different. The coach will bring together the team immediately after the match – those who have played and those on the bench who will play in future games. Together, they will go through a review of the game – the strategy, tactics, teamwork, the good and bad points. Together, they will watch videos, watch them again, review decisions and identify what they could have done differently, making a mental note to build this into future games – especially those against the victorious team this time.

Commitment to learning – immediately

So why is it that in business, all too often we slip into something closer to the primary school model?

Even when we *do* expend time and energy in reviewing a project, or a piece of work – the organisation too often fails to take advantage of its own history.

The trouble with post-project appraisals

Our experience with project close-out reports and post-project appraisal write-ups is that they simply don't get read most of the time. Why is this? Somehow they don't seem to be written with the reader in mind. Somehow they lack timeliness, completeness, passion, even credibility, especially when they become a catalogue of reasons why 'it wasn't anyone's fault'.

According to Sir John Browne, in his 1997 *Harvard Business Review* article, 'Unleashing the Power of Learning':

> *'Most activities or tasks are not one-time events. Whether it's drilling a well or conducting a transaction at a service station, we do the same things repeatedly. Our philosophy is fairly simple: Every time we do something again, we should do it better than the last time'*

What is a retrospect?

In many parts of its business, BP has been using the process described as a *retrospect* as a tool for 'learning after doing'.

A retrospect is a simple meeting, called after the completion of a significant piece of work – at the end of the war, rather than after one of the battles.

Perhaps you have just completed a major product launch, a company reorganisation, a divestment or an acquisition? A retrospect would be relevant in each case.

- It is a way to ensure that a project team feels 'complete'.

- It is a way of transferring lessons immediately to the next similar project, as it is about to start.

- It is a quick and effective way of capturing the knowledge before the team disbands, securing the lessons learned for the benefit of future project teams.

The retrospect meeting lasts from a couple of hours to a couple of days, and requires facilitation. In many ways, the structure resembles that of an AAR:

- Revisit the objectives and deliverables of the project.

- Ask what went well. Ask 'why?' several times.

- Ask what could have gone better. Ask 'why?' several times.

However, unlike an after action review, a retrospect is conducted in more depth – taking anything between an hour for a simple project to up to two days for a complex alliance, involving multiple companies.

More in-depth than an AAR

The other significant difference is that a retrospect is help with the specific intent of capturing lessons and insights for a future project – not just a way for a team to reach 'completion'.

Include the customer!

There is a direct customer for the output of the meeting – indeed, if possible, that customer should be present to pick up the full richness and subtleties of the interactions – subtleties that the capture may well fail to pick up.

Here are the specific steps and facilitator notes that have been successfully applied for over six years in BP.

1.   Call the meeting

It needs to be a face-to-face, meeting. Videoconferencing can be used – it's better than nothing – but a physical meeting is generally more effective. If you are concerned that people will not be open at the meeting, you may also need to conduct one-on-one interviews to supplement this. Don't try and conduct a learning capture by e-mail!

Hold the meeting as soon as you can after the project ends; ideally within a couple of weeks. Memories fade if you leave it much longer, and events become glossed-over, and the past can develop a rose-tinted hue.

Learning events can be celebrations!

Consider positioning the meeting as a celebration if appropriate – this experience from building retail sites in Japan illustrates the point:

'I guess it was successful because the event itself had been a success. It was a very upbeat meeting, so it wasn't seen as a witch-hunt. It was done within the spirit of a celebration – T-shirts were handed out!'

Facilitator's notes:
- *If possible, the venue for the meeting should be closely related to the work environment of the project itself. The project office or 'war-room' is ideal, as it will bring context flooding back for the team.*

- *Avoid neutral or hotel-based locations – this is about capturing the reality of what happened. Sterile hotel conference rooms can lead to sterile conversations!*

- *Allow for approximately 20 minutes per person, or half an hour if it was a lengthy, contentious or complex project.*

- *Ensure that a variety of workshop materials (e.g. Post-It™ notes, flipcharts) are available.*

2. Invite the right people

If a similar project is due to start, or already underway, then there is great value in the new project team attending, so the knowledge can be transferred in real time as soon as it is surfaced.

Include a 'customer' for the lessons whenever possible

The project leader needs to attend, as do key members of the project team. Ideally, the project customer/sponsor/client should attend, at least for the first part of the meeting. However, there is a need to be sensitive to the presence of a highly-placed sponsor at the meeting – it may inhibit some team members.

Ask the project leader/coordinator/manager to schedule the meeting. He or she has most ownership, knows who needs to attend, and still retains some influence in the project team.

In the call to attendees, announce that the purpose of the meeting is to make future projects run more smoothly, by identifying the learning points from this project.

Position the meeting correctly

> If someone in your organisation is about to start a piece of work similar to something that has been recently completed, why not suggest that they use a retrospect as a tool for drawing off the learning points? After all, they have a vested interest.

Below is an example invitation note for a retrospect on a key BP Chemicals acquisition in late 1998 – just prior to the merger with Amoco:

```
I am pleased to confirm the meeting 'Learning from
Styrenix' on 13th November in Antwerp.
```

The purchase of Styrenix was BP's largest acquisition in the Chemicals sector for almost twenty years. Given BP's growth agenda it is possible there will be further acquisitions. It is critical that we take note of the lessons from the integration so that any such future acquisitions have the benefit of what we have experienced and learnt. The BP-Amoco merger is the most immediate application where these lessons could be useful.

The Integration Steering Group asked that we prepare a thorough review of what has been learnt. To help us achieve this I have asked Chris Collison and Barry Smale of BP's Knowledge Management Team to lead us through a process in this one-day workshop.

You can find more information on the Knowledge Management team's work on retrospects (that's what they call what we'll be doing) on the intranet website http://gbc.bpweb.bp.com/km/Tools-techniques/retrospect.htm

More details will follow shortly.

Thanks again for agreeing to attend,

Mike

Facilitator's notes:
- *If a members of a future project team are able to attend, then try to maximise the informal, social time. Split the meeting across two days with room for dinner and bar conversations. Enlarge the coffee breaks at key points in the day; you'll find that once in the same room, people simply cannot stop sharing.*

Independent facilitation is a must!

3.   Appoint a facilitator

You will need a facilitator who was not closely involved in the project, otherwise the meeting may concentrate on 'what we did' rather than 'what should the next team do in similar circumstances'.

If the facilitator is remote from the project, or the subject matter is complex, then she or he may need to do some preparation (e.g. discussions with key players), more in order to understand the hot issues than to understand the content in detail.

The facilitator should also be outside the line-management structure, and the meeting needs to be clearly separate from any personal performance assessment.

Perhaps you're wondering where you might find a facilitator, or what the skills are that you might need to act as a facilitator yourself?

- Get the purpose agreed up front – your role is to do whatever is necessary to help them achieve this.

- Focus on the process rather than the content.

- Watch people's body language – it will tell you more than their words alone.

Facilitator's skills

- Ensure a balanced contribution from all staff – ask questions of the quiet ones.

- Trust your instincts to ask the 'unasked questions'.

- Clarify distinctions between facts and opinions.

- If the purpose of the meeting is not achieved, ask 'what will you do next in order to achieve what you wanted?'

- Get the participants to focus on what actions they should take, rather than on what others should do.

Facilitator's notes:
- *Ask people to introduce themselves and their role. This may feel like overkill for a project team who have been working together over a year, but it can be surprising what can be discovered!*

'This is not about assigning blame or praise – it's about doing even better next time.'

• *Make sure the project team 'owns' the meeting. It's their meeting not yours, hence be prepared to compromise over meeting structure if necessary. The important thing is that all participants gain a fair share of airtime.*

• *Start the meeting by reiterating the purpose – this is not to assign blame or praise but to ensure future projects go even better than this one. Better still, have the project sponsor do this.*

• *Set an atmosphere of openness – if necessary you can introduce 'rules of the game'. There are no right or wrong answers. Affirm that no record of the discussion will be distributed without the agreement of all the participants. Names can always be dissociated from quotes if necessary.*

• *In a big meeting, ask someone to take detailed notes for you, including a verbatim record of key quotes and sound-bites. If you can gain agreement from the participants, consider using a tape recorder, but be very sensitive to the impact of this on the conversation.*

4.   Revisit the objectives and deliverables of the project

This is the point at which you ask 'what did we set out to do?' and 'what did we really achieve?'

Get clear about the original objectives

The facilitator may want to ask the customer or sponsor 'did you get what you wanted?'

It is then valuable to ask if the deadlines were met, and the satisfaction measures achieved.

Facilitator's notes:
• *Try and find the original 'criteria for success' to check whether the project delivered these.*

• *You can ask for original definitions of timescale, cost, resourcing.*

5.   Revisit the project plan or process

In long or complex projects, it can be beneficial to revisit the project plan, compare it with what actually happened, and identify any deviation from the plan.

With the team, construct a flow chart of what happened, identifying tasks, deliverables and decision points. In this way, you can identify those parts of the project that experienced delays or were completed ahead of time, those parts that were particularly efficient or inefficient, and those parts where the team were unclear over what really happened.

Create the 'big picture' if possible

OK. If you've got this far, then the context has been set for a powerful meeting. Silently congratulate yourself before moving onto the next section – this is where the fun starts!

6.   Ask 'what went well?'

Always start with the good points! We should be seeking to build on best practice as much as we are seeking to avoid repeat mistakes.

Start with the good points

Ask 'what were the successful steps towards achieving your objective? What went really well in the project?'

Ask a 'why?' question several times. This will get you to the root of the reason.

Why?

'Our greatest success was hitting that first deadline'

'Why was it that you were able to hit the deadline?'

'We achieved the deadline mainly because we managed to get Jo and Emma working on the design at the last minute.'

'Why Jo and Emma?'

'Well, we had two other pressing projects, but Jo and Emma are a great team, and Jo had worked with BP before so she was able to rework some previous ideas.'

'Why were these ideas relevant this time?'

'We've learned that BP always likes things done in a certain way – we know what works and what doesn't, and we know the design guidelines very well.'

In this example from an Internet site design project, the use of repeated 'why' questioning has developed the success factor from being the ability to meet deadlines into the details of the historical working relationship and availability of guidelines.

Facilitator's notes:

Ensure that all team members participate, involve the quiet ones near to the start

- *Go around the room asking each individual for their successes. Don't let the loud ones dominate the meeting – it is vital that everyone is asked, and heard. Ask the quieter members for their ideas first, to prevent them hiding behind 'I was going to say that too'. The chances are that these insights will be less widely known by the others in the group than the opinions of the more vociferous staff. You may need to give them two minutes thinking time before anyone speaks, to write down what their successes were without being influenced by what others might say.*

- *If time is short, a good ground rule is 'Give me your greatest success factor, the one that made the biggest difference. If someone has already covered it, choose your second greatest.'*

- *It may be good to start with the project leader – they are likely to have the best insight into the details of the project.*

7.   Find out why these aspects went well, and express the learning as advice for the future

Keep the focus on facts, but acknowledge the feelings

Identify the success factors, so that they can be repeated in future.

Try and deal with facts. Feelings need to be acknowledged, but future recommendations have to based on agreed facts.

Ask:

'What repeatable, successful processes did we use?'

Press for specific, repeatable advice

'How could we ensure future projects go just as well, or even better?'

'What would your advice be to future project teams, based on your success here?'

The main task here is to keep pressing for specific, repeatable advice.

Facilitator's notes:

- *This part of the meeting will be a conversation. You have two options. The first is to ask the probing questions (and let the conversation develop) as each person identifies their success factor(s). The idea is to reach group consensus advice through conversation. In a close team this will happen naturally.*

- *An alternative approach, useful if the team is more subdued, is to identify all the issues first, then choose the ones to work on as a team.*

Almost certainly, as discussion continues, 'bad' points as well as good will be discussed. Don't try and stifle this, let the discussion continue as far as consensus advice, then return to the next person's success factor. Asking for success factors is just a way to get the topics into the room, and should not be used to stifle discussion if the negatives creep in.

8. Then, ask 'what could have gone better?'

There are bound to be some areas where things could have gone better, where pitfalls were identified too late, and where process was sub-optimal.

Even successes have room for improvement

Ask 'what were the aspects that stopped you delivering even more?'

Avoid letting people 'make others wrong' – rather, encourage them to say 'my view of the incident was different'. Remember that everyone's perception is equally valid.

Facilitator's notes:

- *Again, go round the room and ask each individual. It often makes sense to start with the team leader, who you have already asked to set the tone in being open. If he/she admits that 'things could have gone better', or more powerfully 'I could have done these things better', the rest of the team will open up too.*

9. Find out what the difficulties were

Identify the stumbling blocks and pitfalls, so they can be avoided in future. The following questions are useful:

• 'Given the information and knowledge we had at the time, what could we have done better?'

• 'Given the information and knowledge we have now, what are we going to do differently in similar situations in future, to ensure success?'

• 'What would your advice be to future project teams, based on your experiences here?'

Facilitator's notes:
• *You have to ensure that this section of the process does not become a witchhunt or a finger-pointing exercise. It is OK to let people have their say, but rather than let them focus on the past ask 'So what would you do differently next time?'*

• *Consider writing on a flip chart: 'So what about next time?' to remind people of the focus of the meeting.*

• *Again you have the option to hold the discussion as each person identifies their points, or to collect the points and choose which to discuss.*

10. Ensure that the participants leave the meeting with their feelings acknowledged

You do not want anyone to leave the meeting feeling that things were covered up, or that valuable effort was not acknowledged.

Access to this can be achieved by asking people for a numerical rating of the project. Ask, 'looking back, how satisfied are you with

this project; marks out of ten?' Many people will say 'the project was fine, no problems' and still give it eight out of ten. This enables you to ask 'what would have made it a ten for you?' and so access residual feelings of dissatisfaction.

Sometimes you might want them to reflect on the impact of the process on the result – it's possible to still achieve a great outcome via an imperfect process.

Facilitator's notes:
- *It is worth giving them five seconds of thinking time to write down their score before asking them to call it out, so they are not influenced by other people's ratings.*

11.   'What next?'

If the project team is going straight on to a similar project, it is useful to follow the retrospect with a planning session for this.

> *Couple a retrospect to a planning meeting*

Facilitator's notes:
- *If the previous project went badly, it will be worth reminding the team that they will need to act on the knowledge they have just uncovered, if they want future projects to run more smoothly. Ideally they should embed the knowledge into revised team processes, procedures or structure.*

- *Press for people to commit to actions, particularly on the big difficult issues!*

> *Press for actions!*

- *If there was dissatisfaction in the room – perhaps someone felt a lack of acknowledgment – there may be steps that could be taken to address this even at this late stage in a project.*

12.   Recording the meeting

It is vital to have an interesting and well-structured account of the meeting and its outcomes. A suggested framework is:

- guidelines for the future;

- history from the project to illustrate the guidelines;

- names of the people involved, for future reference; and

- any key artefacts (e.g. documents, project plans).

Quotes are the lifeblood of the written account

This determines what you need to record from the meeting. The direct use of quotes is one of the most powerful ways of capturing the depth of feeling – and of creating a summary that is likely to be read.

> 'Nothing turns me off more than a ten-page report full of abstracted motherhood statements – I can already feel my eyes beginning to close ...'
>
> Chris Collison

You see? Sprinkle selected quotes liberally throughout the write-up. Quotes should be attributed to a person wherever possible. It goes without saying that the person attributed with any quote will need to agree to its inclusion.

Recom-mendations are the best way to summarise the lessons learned

Also record as accurately as possible what the recommendations are for the future. Often the recommendations won't be clearly stated in the meeting, and the facilitator will need to do some rewording of the meeting records. Express the recommendations as clearly, measurably and unambiguously as possible.

The acid test of the document's usefulness is to ask yourself 'if I were to be the next project leader, would these lessons be any use to me?'.

Circulate everything for agreement before going wider

Ensure that you circulate the write-up around the participants for comment. Make sure nobody was misquoted, and that the facilitator's wording of the lessons really reflects the views of the team.

Once agreed, distribute the final copy to the team. Consider also who else could benefit from the content and send it to them.

What if a project was just starting up in three years time – how would the team be prompted to read your record of events? The final stage is to find somewhere logical to store this invaluable document – somewhere where it will get read in detail and applied to future projects. Somewhere a group of people will review it and treat it as an asset to be embedded into future company processes and guidelines.

Make it available as the basis for something even more powerful ...

The last three chapters have shown ways of generating learning – learning before, during and after. But how do we find the right people to learn from?

FINDING THE RIGHT PEOPLE
– IF ONLY I KNEW WHO

Everything that we have discussed in the book so far depends heavily on people connecting with people. But how do you ensure that the *right* people connect?

In this chapter:

- The importance of managing know-who, and stimulating connections between people.

- Why personal home pages are a powerful foundation for knowledge sharing.

- How to create and introduce a successful knowledge directory.

Unnatural actions

Louise teaches six-year-olds in a primary school in West London – close to Heathrow Airport. Each morning, just before starting their work, the class participates in an activity known as 'brain gym'. All of the children perform 'unnatural actions' such as folding their arms, then folding them in a counter-intuitive way. If you are right-handed, you will naturally place your right forearm over your left – try left over right. Other activities involve 'simultaneously patting your head and rubbing your chest', and reciting the alphabet whilst moving alternate arms and legs. It's a hilarious sight at times, but brain-gym is more than a humorous icebreaker.

Creating the connections that improve learning performance

Accelerated learning theory suggests that such actions stimulate the left and right hand side of the brain simultaneously, creating neural connections across the 'corpus callosum'. The end result of this increased neural activity is that each child is *more receptive to learning.*

What has accelerated learning theory got to do with knowledge management?

If you consider teams, divisions, business units or even newly-merged companies, there is a tendency for knowledge to align itself with organisational constructs. When this is the case, learning is likely to occur in parallel – in ignorance of what another part of the organisation is doing.

In our case, BP and Amoco were like the left and right-hand sides of the brain. The immediate post-merger challenge was the creation of an environment where relationships were forced beyond their natural boundaries – stimulating the breakdown and recreation of networks and communities, and encouraging staff to think beyond their normal circles of influence. In this way, learning could occur by the connections between both sides of the brain, or organisation.

Think about when you first came to work for your current organisation. How long did it take you to develop the relationships, contacts and networks that you now have. You might even want to draw a map of these.

Creating the environment to enable connections

So how do you create such an environment? An environment that puts you in touch with people who *know*?

Making connections requires more than the mechanical bringing together of the right people. Unlike neurons in the brain, people exhibit more complex behaviour! A desire to learn and the willingness to share need to be present for a truly effective connection to occur.

BP took a bottom-up approach, to develop a knowledge directory that gained the buy-in of many thousands of staff. The product was known as 'Connect'.

Connect took the form of a searchable intranet repository, through which all staff could search for people with relevant knowledge and experience. Additionally, they could easily create a personal home page rich in content, which in turn would be accessible to anyone with network access.

Learning before doing

Investing some time learning before from other corporate, Yellow-Pages initiatives proved to be time well spent for Connect. We held a peer assist (see Chapter 6, Learning from your Peers) with staff at Microsoft, Glaxo Wellcome, Schlumberger, Hughes Space and Communications and Proctor & Gamble, which yielded the following findings:

- keep the vision clear;

- manage the relationship with the HR department; and

- ensure that ownership lies with individuals.

> *Three key lessons from the experiences of others*

Let's look at these in a little more detail.

Have a clear vision

What is the underlying vision of what we are trying to achieve here?

What is distinctive about a corporate Yellow Pages relative to other directories or resource planning systems?

In our case, we were striving for an environment where all employees could easily search for people with the expertise they sought. All of them could create and maintain a personal home page on the intranet.

Generating ten minute telephone calls is where the value lies.

What would then follow would be a series of conversations between the searcher and the resulting staff – perhaps little more than a ten minute telephone call. Enough of a conversation to prevent a wheel being re-invented, help share a successful insight, or a nugget of key commercial intelligence.

The transfer of knowledge is all about people and relationships rather than projects and resources – hence environment to support knowledge management needs to respect people as people, present them as people and provide ways for them to key into relationships with others.

Complementing, not competing with HR systems

This is not the traditional realm of HR systems, which exist for a different purpose. The information in such systems tends to be owned by the personnel department.

For such a *knowledge management* system to be successful, our experience is that ownership needs to reside with the individuals concerned. This is their personal, alternative prospectus – how they want to be known, rather than how the company knows them. As such, it complements existing people systems rather than replaces them. It helps build a living, breathing, three-dimensional representation of a person – far broader than a set of work histories or training records.

In summary, creating an employee-owned knowledge directory is a laudable aim, and one which others will be quick to exploit. Expect to be approached by people with their own agendas who will be keen to 'enhance' your environment beyond all recognition through a series of minor additions.

The bottom line is that if you don't want your knowledge directory to get railroaded by the staff development committee, resource managers, HR professionals or, worse still, the IT department working on the latest and greatest 'mother of all directories' ... then practise your defence!

Everyone will want a piece of the action!

Perhaps you're thinking '*That's all very well for large corporations, but what about my company of 50, or even 500 staff – do I really need such a system?*'

For 50 people, you probably don't. You probably know everyone in the company fairly well. But do you know them well enough to know what they need? You might consider a simple approach, even paper-based, where staff can post their offers of assistance and requests for help. This may reveal some unexpectedly hidden talents, and liberate a new, informal marketplace for knowledge.

Knowledge directories in small companies

For 500 people, especially where they are split across more than one office, then some form of a system will be a valuable resource. Something that simply lists what people know about and what help they need, linked to their contact details, could make a big difference. The authors are aware of several small companies who rely on systems similar to Connect in their sophistication.

The value of personal information

A consultant colleague often quotes the phrase:

'There's no such thing as strictly business – everything is personal.'
Brad Meyer

Isn't this is the reason why golf clubs flourish? Isn't that the basis on which salespeople operate?

If this maxim holds true, then the ramifications for the content of any knowledge directories are significant. Remember, our vision is to generate ten minute conversations that act as the catalysts for effective knowledge exchange. Think back to the last time you had a ten minute conversation

Business relationships flourish when personal details are shared

with someone. Perhaps it was on a flight or at a conference? What sort of things you might cover during that ten minutes?

- Where do you work?

- What is your job?

OK, fairly mundane so far. So we continue looking for common ground?

Work-related information is only the tip of the iceberg

- Do you know James, I think he used to work in your head office?

- Did you go to that conference in St. Andrews?

- Do you play golf?

- What's your handicap?

- What about your partner, does he/she play too?'

- Do you have children? How many of each?

Let's stop here and look at what's happening. We're spiralling out from the conventional work-related areas, and looking to connect at deeper levels – through shared experiences, social similarities and emotional challenges.

Now, go back ten minutes and imagine that you already knew the answers to those questions. How much easier is it now to establish trust and a working relationship with this person?

Now imagine that you had instant access to this level of knowledge about everyone in your organisation. That's powerful. And that's why creating space for people to express the less formal side of their lives is so important to any knowledge directory.

It's almost as if you can know a person before you meet or speak with them.

People's Connect pages may contain an enormous variety of 'soft' information. The following three excerpts illustrate this:

> 'I have two great kids that I like spending time with while they still like spending it with me. We are very involved in our Church. I enjoy hunting and fishing with my 13 year old son. He enjoys fishing, so we fish. We went for five days, way out in the wilderness, on a float-fishing trip in Alaska last summer. I enjoy supervising a good team of engineers and I like having a great time doing so. I like delivering big projects like Schiehallion when I was the Wells Team Leader there.'

The power of knowing people before meeting them

> 'I think it's a good idea to continue through life learning new skills, although I think both my piano teacher and Spanish teacher wish I'd give up trying!'

> 'I'm married with a three-year-old daughter, Martha, who occupies most of my free time, and we have another on the way! I live 3 miles from Sunbury, in Shepperton – pretty close to the Red Lion Pub and the river! If you're turned-on by personality profiling, I'm: ENFP (Myers Briggs), Plant/Resource Investigator (Belbin), Creator Innovator (TMI).'

What is in Connect?

A summary of the ingredients of a typical Connect home page.

- Name

- Job title

- Team business unit

- Free text area

The ingredients of a typical 'Connect' home page

- Structured taxonomy of 'areas of expertise'

- Languages spoken

- Internal and external contacts

- Favourite web links (internal and external)

- Uploaded photograph

- Uploaded *résumé* (CV)

- Uploaded audio clip

- Membership of networks and communities of practice

- Basic contact information – including telephone numbers, e-mail addresses etc.

The process for creating these rich pages is supported by templates, *very* simple templates! Nobody needs to write HTML, or to even know what it stands for – just the ability to think, type and click, and most importantly of all, the willingness to be contacted.

I don't know what to write!

This is a common complaint for a variety of reasons. For some, natural modesty is the barrier. Others find it hard to précis appropriately. A commonly observed phenomenon is 'writer's block false start'.

Freeform text is valuable and needs to be encouraged by the right questions

With the best of intentions, the author starts with a sentence or two, stalls, and then becomes distracted. Faced with the prospect of leaving a part-finished page, the author falls victim to a self-imposed culture of perfection, and deletes what he or she has already written, under the self-conscious misapprehension that it is better to say nothing, than to say something incomplete.

In order to help overcome this, Connect prompts the writer with the following open questions.

- What are you currently working on?

- What areas have you worked on in the past?

- What subjects might you like to be contacted about?

- What do you enjoy doing?

- Is there any help that you need?

Some staff work through these questions in a structured manner, whilst others use them as prompts for ideas. In either case, the resultant page has thoughtful content, owned by the individual.

During the credibility-building stages of the project, professional coaches were employed to floor-walk and help staff through the process of constructing their page, including the freeform areas. Whilst effective in securing high quality content, we were unable to scale-up the approach satisfactorily. However, the good examples created during this phase serves as 'seeds' for others struggling for inspiration

Direct support and coaching can produce high quality content.

A picture is worth a thousand words

About a third of BP staff have provided a picture of themselves. Many of these are your regular head-and-shoulders, passport-style shots – very useful for identification, but not as informative as they could be.

By far the more interesting images are the more personal, human interest shots. Family groups, staff standing proudly beside their treasured cabriolet, private plane, caravan(!), or even vintage motorcycle. Action shots of people skiing, image-enhanced morphing animations, Disney cartoons, baby pictures, pet-poses, even the odd glamour shot – albeit well within the bounds of absolute decency – are just some examples.

Informal photographs create a three dimensional picture of the person. Head and shoulders shots are for passports!

The award for 'most innovative photo' goes to Dave, who embedded real-time shots of him working at his desk via a static camera, which updates every two minutes. Not only can you read all about Dave's detailed experience, background and hobbies – you can assess whether now is a good time to call him by the expression on his face, or the current level of his coffee cup.

Some day soon all this will be mundane, but for now, 'Dave-cam' is a great source of amusement for those who happen upon it unsuspectingly.

Principles for a successful knowledge directory

Devolved ownership. The system was to require minimal central administration, and to occur as a part of the infrastructure owned by everyone. Only the individuals concerned could update their pages – not their line managers, team secretaries or the HR department – just the individuals themselves. The content was to be non-validated – it is assumed that staff would be honest in the information they provided.

From a process perspective, we wanted our approach to be entirely voluntary – without the negative backlash or grudging compliance that management edict can generate. A simple environment based on trust.

Voluntary and non-validated; a truly employee-owned approach

To be crystal clear: *this is not about HR information systems, and not about resource management for six-month projects. It is about generating ten minute telephone conversations and tapping into a vein of human nature that produces the response – 'Even though I've never heard of you, because you have approached me with a request for help, I'll give you ten minutes of my time'.*

On reflection, perhaps this *is* a form of resource management, but resource in this paradigm is the latent intellectual resource of the organisation, and management's ability to mobilise and harness what is already known.

The structure–freedom equation

Stop for a minute and think about your e-mail inbox.

Perhaps you have a well-ordered hierarchy of sub-folders, and fastidiously keep your inbox empty – 'a place for everything and everything in its place'. Roughly a third of people work in this manner.

Perhaps you keep all your e-mails in a huge single folder and sort, search and filter in order to retrieve what you need. One in ten tend to work this way.

Provide for different working styles – structure and freedom both have their place in a knowledge directory

You probably fit somewhere between these two extremes. People are comfortable working with different levels of structure. Some find it constraining, some find it liberating.

This translates directly into the realm of knowledge directories. Many people would blanch at the prospect of filling a blank sheet of paper with a story about themselves. Some would rebel at the prospect of ticking the boxes that relate to them.

The common sense solution then, is to provide an environment which caters for both preferences – life's box-tickers as well as life's lyricists. Any knowledge directory which builds implicit exclusion into its design is likely to be self-defeating.

The technological implications of this are significant. The power of any search technology is reliant on a common way of describing the same concept – a common language or taxonomy. By equipping the user community with a detailed pick-list of terms, an implicit common language is created.

Maintain an inclusive approach in the design – or risk losing part of your audience

'*Give me the names and faces of all the Chicago-based French-speakers with expertise in negotiating and e-commerce.*'

Trivial. Relational databases have had this capability for years. However, to rely exclusively on structured 'database' searches presupposes that all potential requirements can be captured within a simple taxonomy.

'*Find me everyone who has any relationship with Chevron*'

'*Find me people with a passion for fly fishing*'

These ad-hoc queries require more general free-text searches. Again, providing for both requirements is the best way to engage a broad base of staff in using a knowledge directory.

The Connect project

Everybody believed in the idea, but nobody had made it happen

Connect was an opportunity always waiting to happen, but one which required a degree of coordination. Prior to its first incarnation in late 1997, there were no less than twelve independent 'who's who?' directories at BP. Each one served its own community and there was no collective effort to align or integrate these islands of information, or even transfer the requirements, or lessons learned, from one system to the next.

When a thirteenth directory showed signs of appearing, it was time to find a more intelligent way of tackling this business need. A peer assist workshop was arranged, and for the first time, a specification for a system that had the potential to satisfy the needs of the entire organisation.

Gaining buy-in from some of the most senior staff sent a powerful signal to the organisation. Naturally, Sir John Browne was already known to every employee. However, the fact that he agreed to have a home page with photograph, career history and some informal information about his hobbies and interests sent a strong message to the company that he implicitly supported the initiative. Even if you have to prepare a printed example in advance in order to ease the way with the support staff that typically surround senior executives, the payback is worthwhile. Negotiate tenaciously!

Buy in from the top of the organisation is well worth persevering for

A prototype was created, based around the requirements of a pilot community of 500 technical staff, staff whose leadership had generously agreed to investing in a tool that had the potential to serve the entire organisation. This pilot phase was used to test the principles and technology. Changes were fed back into the design throughout this time, and additional small focus groups were used to broaden the design critique. Within six months the number of people with Connect home pages had grown to over 1000. At this point, with a credible set of early adopters, a concerted internal marketing campaign was initiated.

Bring together the potential and existing stakeholders and engage them in the design of the future

Persuading several thousand staff to each spend 15 minutes creating a personal home page is a non-trivial exercise. Given the underlying philosophy that this was to be a non-mandatory, bottom-up initiative, the most effective way of delivering Connect as a company-wide environment was to deliver through others.

Connect 'champions' were informally recruited as part of the underground campaign – staff from any background who believed in its potential, and were willing to give a few hours of their time to promote it within their own business unit or network.

Thirty staff volunteered to run local marketing initiatives – ranging from traditional presentations, 'donut talks' and exhibition stands

Make use of local volunteers, and their innovative ideas wherever possible

with digital cameras and scanners, through to competitions between teams, with champagne for the first team to be 'fully connected', and some highly innovative local approaches. In Alaska, the two-litre milk cartons that graced the staff restaurant were embellished with 'wanted posters' that carried the photograph of a local employee, with a few words describing their background or experience. The implicit challenge to the breakfasters was to go back to their desks and use Connect to identify the face that they had been staring at over their cornflakes.

Make use of tokens for recognition, however trivial the cost

A thousand 'Connect pens' were purchased, and used to great effect as token recognition from the project leader for staff who set good examples. An encouraging and grateful e-mail was sent to such a page owner, notifying them that a pen was on its way to them. The e-mail finished with a request to tell other staff in their areas about Connect, and yielded great rewards – up to a hundredfold. Many Connect champions were drawn in through this simple process – all from the investment of a $5 pen!

Regardless of the culture, stories are a consistently powerful way to augment a marketing campaign, and using anecdotes to illustrate the power of a tool like Connect has been highly successful.

Consider the following example, taken from a note from a marketing manager in Tanzania to a Connect champion in Singapore.

From: Mondoloka, Fumu

Sent: 07 July 1998 15:18

To: Abrahams, Andrea D (Singapore)

Subject: RE: Does it work?

Andrea,

Connect is a brilliant tool!

Success stories are the most powerful marketing material

To walk you through the highlights of the breweries story:

I had a calling to innovate an offer for Tanzania Breweries which is under South African Breweries and we do not exactly have all the SAB accounts in the region. BP (Tanzania) put in a bid and are tipped to be awarded but we have to get the business and lock it up.

I searched on Connect for Sector expertise pulled a few names and sent an e-mail detailing my request. To my amazement the spiral of help the process yielded was incredible. We got from the network a blue print of an offer made to a Scottish Brewery which we might not implement in its form but is a sound basis for us to kit one together.

My colleagues from Tanzania and I are currently assessing what we can draw from it and I should travel to Dar es Salaam in two weeks to gather with the guys there the information we need then we'll zero in on the offer.

No proof of the pudding yet but we shall certainly share it with every one that helped when we know the deal is done, which I am sure is going to be soon.

Fumu

Incidentally, the deal *did* get done.

This story can be read online as part of Connect, together with ten others. Having a distributed network of local champions made it relatively easy to get a flow of examples and stories to pass on to others, and to write-up for internal magazines and presentations.

E-mail signature files have virus-like capacity to spread – make use of them!

In each case, Connect was promoted as fun, alternative and individual. And it worked!

E-mail jokes have a capacity to spread, virus-like, across an organisation. During the summer of 1998, someone, somewhere in BP decided to create the following e-mail signature, which included a link to their Connect page:

I'm connected: *http://connect.bpweb.bp.com/searchid=82025*
Are you? *http://connect.bpweb.bp.com*

Within a few months, the signature file had been copied and customised by thousands of staff.

Knowing where to start

Find a starting place in the organisation that will yield quick wins

Choosing the right pilot community is critical to the early success of a knowledge directory, so where is the most fertile soil to begin sowing the seeds?

In piloting and launching Connect, we found four different indicators that were consistent with rapid uptake.

- *Staff who have clear internal customers.* This included internal consultants, HR and IT professionals, shared service groups and technologists. Anybody who has a need to be visible to a constituency is likely to view tools like Connect as a positive vehicle for their own agenda.

- *Staff who work in geographically dispersed teams, networks and communities.* Because of the global nature of BP's business, many teams work across several locations. More significantly, networks and communities of practice have strong roles to play in sharing know-how, but meet very infrequently. In both cases, through learning more about a remote colleague's background, seeing their picture and understanding more about their immediate environment, relationships are strengthened. With the right level of coordination, tools like Connect can be used as effective distributed ice-breakers.

- *Businesses which are geographically remote.* BP operates in over 100 countries worldwide, including some inhospitable environments. At times, the distance can lead frontier teams into attempted self-sufficiency, sub-optimal performance and personal frustration. Positioning Connect as a way of remaining attached to the body of the company and tapping into the resources of tens of thousands of staff is easy with such groups, and the quid pro quo of individuals making themselves available as well as asking for help, follows quickly.

- *Businesses or departments with new leadership.* When leadership is renewed, the relationship-building process usually needs to start all over again. Some leaders saw Connect as an ideal way for them to visualise and begin to informally 'know' their staff. Others make a habit of bringing up someone's Connect page before talking to them on the telephone in order to have more effective conversations.

Embedding into business processes

The final part of the marketing strategy was to target some of the core people processes for the company. Staff joining and leaving, and staff development training in particular.

Business processes can be used as powerful prompts

As part of the induction process, new recruits in BP are introduced to Connect and encouraged to use it to extend their networks and introduce themselves to others.

Conversely, when leaving the company, staff are entitled to delegate ownership of their page to a colleague who is remaining inside BP as a fragment of corporate memory, and as a potential calling card.

Finally, staff attending some leadership development courses are encouraged to find out about their fellow attendees through their entries in Connect. These reminders serve to institutionalise the usage of Connect, and spread the word.

Providing valuable context by linking information with its owner

In addition to answering the 'Who knows about…?' questions, a web-based collection of personal home pages has a large secondary benefit.

Because all staff with entries in Connect have a unique URL, each page can then be linked to, from other web pages and applications.

Link information to the people who know

This is a powerful benefit as it enables web content to be linked to individuals in a context rich way. Traditionally, web pages might contain a 'mailto:' link at the foot of each page linking the content to an owner.

Why do people search the web – intranet, extranet, Internet for information? What do you expect as a return on your invested time, beyond the sheer entertainment of searching and finding?

- For some people the expected outcome is hard information – give me something that I can print off and act upon with confidence.

- For others, it will be a set of leads for further research – using the information landscape as a brainstorming environment.

- For the remainder it might be a set of contacts to pursue for further information, of to confirm the information that has already been provided.

Where the quality of the information can't always be guaranteed – often the case in large corporate intranets that have grown organically – the integrity of the owner contact information can be as valuable as the content itself. As a broad generalisation, this scenario is a representation of BP's intranet at the time of writing.

The content is essentially an advertisement for a conversation with the owner.

In these cases, being able to switch instantly from reading the *content* to reading about the *author*, through a single click of the mouse, is of tremendous value. This extra context increases the likelihood of a conversation taking place, and may improve the effectiveness of that conversation as a vehicle for knowledge transfer.

Intranets can be used as places to meet people, as well as find information

Here's an example.

Anne is searching the intranet for information relating to business in Azerbaijan. She discovers a page authored two years previously by Bob, and wonders whether the commercial climate has changed during the elapsed two years. She clicks on the e-mail link on the page and starts to write Bob a mail.

Half way through, she starts to feel a bit foolish – like a cold-caller, and considers backing out, or taking the information at face value. However, she perseveres, completes and sends the note.

Since Bob moved location six months ago, and his e-mail address changed, Anne's attempt bounces, and the effort is wasted.

Personal home pages provide the context behind the information

Here's another take on the same example.

Anne is searching the intranet for information relating to business in Azerbaijan. She discovers a page authored two years previously by Bob, and wonders whether the commercial climate has changed during the elapsed two years. She clicks on the link on the page that links to Bob's personal home page, looks thoughtfully at his photograph and starts to read all about him.

Half way through, she discovers that like her, he has experience in integrated marketing. Encouraged by this, she checks his contact details and telephones him, noting that he returned to Aberdeen earlier in the year.

Anne and Bob now have two children and live on the outskirts of Edinburgh.

OK, so the last bit is stretching the point a little! However, this example illustrates the power of relatedness between individuals and the value of photographs and autobiography to help generate this.

In BP today, many thousands of intranet pages link to Connect pages – names in business unit organigrams, group photographs, page owner links all redirect to people's personal home pages.

All this sounds a little mundane, but it represents a significant shift in how people approach their information resources. BP's intranet is now a place where you 'meet people' rather than just 'find information'. Context as well as content; know-who as well as know-how.

To close the chapter – now that you've finished patting your head and rubbing your chest – here are the ten key lessons that were learned during the two-year Connect initiative:

- maintain a clear and distinctive vision and positioning;

- personal ownership is the only way;

Ten key lessons learned from two years of a successful initiative

- balance between informal and formal;

- photographs make all the difference;

- ensure that your product design is inclusive;

- start with a customer-facing pilot;

- deliver through local enthusiasts;

- use success stories as a marketing tool;

- leadership by example, not edict; and

- embed into people processes.

Whilst a tool like Connect enables the creation of a transient set of contacts, more permanent and formal networks play an equally important part sharing knowledge. The next chapter explores the vital role of networks and communities of practice as both the guardians and channels of a company's knowledge.

NETWORKING AND COMMUNITIES OF PRACTICE

10

In the last chapter we talked about how we stay connected with those who know, in order to have a ten-minute conversation at the right time.

In this chapter we will take a look at:

- Why people find the time to help others.

- Some definitions.

- Being part of the community.

- Launching a community.

- Sustaining a community.

- Networks as the guardians of the company's knowledge.

I t was 3 February. Somewhere in the control room at a refinery in Australia, John – a plant inspector – was planning the inspection schedule for the following week. He sent an e-mail requesting some advice from his network about the inspec- *Networks ...* tion of fan blades and hubs on cooling fan units. By 11 a.m. the following morning Steve, an inspector at Salt Lake City Refinery, had responded with some reports of repeated hub failures in 1985, 1989 and again in 1997. The gist of the report was that it was due to the U-bolts that hold the blades to the hub not being properly tightened. After holding discussions with the manufacturer, the procedure manual was amended to recommend installing a protective guard and performing preventative maintenance at 6–12-month intervals.

On 7 February a network member passed this advice on to a larger network in the exploration and production stream of the business. One member of this network passed it on to a further hundred people he felt ought to know. One of these sent it to his local team of twenty maintenance engineers and so on ...

... taking and applying the learning

John the inspector in Australia took heed of the recommendations, and he was not the only one. By 30 March, the Hemphill Gas plant in Texas, as a result of the warning, had inspected 16 fan units even though they were of a different manufacture. They found several nuts not tightened to the proper specs and four blades worn beyond repair. They circulated pictures of the damage by e-mail. As a result of this inspection they reviewed their maintenance procedures.

No less than three management acknowledgements were received complimenting Hemphill on taking and applying the learning.

On 4 April, Steve – the Salt Lake City inspector who had sent the advice – was sent the string of e-mail notes to let him see the wider benefit of his providing the recommendations, thus reinforcing the good behaviour.

Why people find time to help others

Achieving more with less people

The restructuring and delayering of organisations such as BP have created flatter, more business-focused companies. More gets achieved with less people. The experts sit within individual teams and businesses and are focused on delivering the objectives of their team or business. No team has the luxury of having an expert for everything they need to know. So how can we access the knowledge across the organisation? We learned in the last chapter how to find out who knows, but how do we go about getting them to help and why should they?

In the story above, the request and the solution were disseminated quickly and effectively, not to a single circulation or to a particular expert but to a series of linked, pre-existing networks. Consider if you know 50 people who can help you do your work? If each of them knows 50 others (only half of whom are duplicates) then pretty soon you have access to a large number of people and a large amount of knowledge.

Within BP there are more than 250 networks, nobody knows exactly how many, as the number is always changing. Some are formal and have clear goals, others are very informal and help develop the capability of individuals.

Knowledge is not evenly distributed

Frequently the knowledge we need to do our job exists somewhere within the organisation, though it is not evenly distributed. Sometimes we may not know what we don't know.

BP has gained a lot of value by sharing what it knows as well as by importing external good practices. That value is captured by applying leading practices in a small number of our businesses.

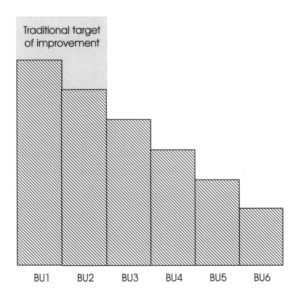

Traditional target of improvement

BU1 BU2 BU3 BU4 BU5 BU6

We find there is a lot more value in identifying a good practice and applying it rapidly across a large number of teams and businesses to bring each to a high standard of performance. So, imagine someone works out how to increase the productivity of a particular process that saves £10,000. If we can apply that fifty times, the company saves £500,000. We do not mandate the change; rather the network of practitioners sees the sense in making the change to improve their own performance. They would be foolish not to. They would become uncompetitive.

Quick wins come from sharing what we already know

Whilst everyone should be looking to innovate and to create new, higher standards of performance, the quick wins are likely to come from sharing what we already know somewhere in our organisation.

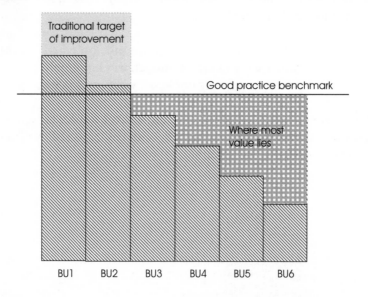

'*No traditional corporate structure, regardless of how decluttered and delayered, can muster up the speed, flexibility and focus that success today demands. Networks are faster, smarter and more flexible ...*'

Charan, 1991

It has taken a while for us to understand how to make this happen.

Take a few minutes to think about a time when you were part of an effective network inside or outside your organisation. What made it successful? How did it feel to be a member? How did you interact with other members?

Defining networks and communities

We would like to offer a few definitions and distinctions. We've confused ourselves frequently enough through using the same words to mean different things.

One thing that we are not talking about here is the wire that links our computers together! We are talking about groups of individuals sharing because they have a common interest in motorbikes; or the mutual dependency created by living on a remote island; a colony of ants that work together to feed and protect their community.

Networks of people are of many sorts and we give them a multitude of names. Communities operate through mutual benefit, across the normal organisational structures. At the simplest level they have few needs: a common sense of purpose, a means of communication, a good coordinator, and the autonomy to run themselves.

One classification that we have found useful is, communities of interest, practice, or commitment.

- *Communities of interest* are collections of individuals who have a mutual interest in a particular topic, often peripheral to work. Examples are sports clubs, hobby groups, charity circles.

Communities of interest, of practice, and of commitment

- *Communities of practice (or enabling networks)* build and apply the same practices, negotiate which methods work best how and when they are most useful. They are the guardians of competence in that practice within the company. They help each other to develop the competence to contribute individually within their business units.

- *Communities of commitment (or delivery networks)* have a much harder edge. They have some clear business goal and the network is collectively accountable for delivery. Frequently these networks are a subgroup of communities of practice and have a fixed life, until what they are aiming for is delivered.

Within BP, we focus on the second and third types of networks, and we have called them enabling networks and delivery networks.

The two types of networks are similar in many respects, but are distinguished based on the *measurable value* they provide to the business and *formality of structure*. Delivery networks have a high degree of structure to ensure that we capture the measurable value.

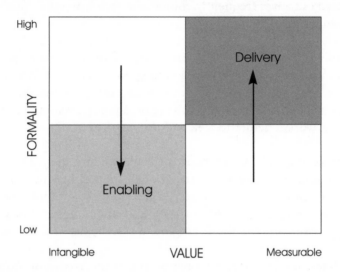

Delivery

The purpose of a *delivery network* is to deliver a common objective by pooling knowledge and translating it into actions that improve business results. BP has some clear targets on reducing Greenhouse gas emissions for example. The Green Operations network shares knowledge across the organisation so the separate businesses can deliver the targeted reduction. The individuals in the network may collaborate across business boundaries. This is a delivery network.

BP establishes delivery networks when a significant gap between the value of current practice and recognised good practice is noticed. Capturing the full value from the network generally requires crossing organisation, discipline, or geographic boundaries.

The first step is to find a coordinator, who will effectively lead the group to deliver the business objective. The network has a representative business customer and also a mentor to provide assurance and coaching.

Green Operations network

The goal of the Green Operations network is to identify, create and implement new ideas to make our operations more environmentally friendly. It facilitates company-wide communication with both managers and engineers. It currently has 575 members, some of whom are passive watchers, and a core who actively ask questions or join in the dialogue in an electronic discussion forum. There are 10–15 questions a month with an average of six responses to each. There is a full time facilitator who ensures that the questions are answered and that the key know-how is captured.

The network is focused around its own intranet site, which reminds them of their purpose, goals, membership and key knowledge. It is also focused by a business management steering group, who set the challenges and priorities. The website keeps the community aware of current issues and key projects. Knowledge transfer is also supported by specialist teams, workshops, newsletters, videos, webcasts, reports, links with academic institutions and technology companies.

The network has a performance contract with the business sponsor who may be acting on behalf of several businesses. The members of a delivery network are nominated to ensure the right expertise and representation is included.

... and enabling

Enabling networks on the other hand improve the performance of the individual members by sharing internal and external knowledge and good practices. This enables them to impact their business performance. They are defined around the *discipline* they are about, by knowledge rather than *task*. The emphasis is on building capacity for that discipline within the company. Enabling networks can be as valuable or more valuable than delivery networks. However it is harder to measure that value. We have frequently found that efforts to formalise or measure the benefits, jeopardise the livelihood of the network.

The three dimensional modelling (3D Mod) network is a good example of an enabling network.

3D Mod network

3D Mod is a network of practitioners of a variety of disciplines, all of whom aim to understand the performance of a subsurface oil reservoir. Three-dimensional reservoir modelling is a technique to improve the detail of reservoir description, since this leads to better reservoir management. It has been running for a number of years and has a coordinator, Ray King, who energises the network in his spare time. He has a full-time job delivering to one of the business units. The members rarely meet, but they help each other develop their capability to deliver within their own business. They do this by sharing what they know, and also by collectively pushing the boundaries of their shared discipline.

Most of the sharing is via a discussion group in MS Exchange. The discussion group is a distribution list and a companion public folder on Exchange. Material posted in the folder is automatically sent to people on the distribution list. In addition the folder is open to everyone with Exchange access (all employees plus many contractors), even if they are not on the list. So an individual can choose to be prompted when there is something new, or look at the folder on an occasional basis.

'I wanted to build on a habit they had in their daily routine, the e-mail habit' says Ray. 'People can participate in the discussion or can view the contents of the forum without committing to being on the list'.

Members send messages to the folder ranging from technical queries, bug fixes, requests for help, to debates on good practices. The folder receives around 30 messages a month. Ray acts as a moderator, keeping the discussion alive and encouraging debate.

The membership is currently at 99 and, except for an increase after the BP–Amoco merger, numbers have remained steady for the last six years. There is a significant turnover of members, people join it when it is useful to them and leave it when it's not. Measured over one two-year period, half of the members changed.

After the first year or two more than 800 messages were still in the folder, unsorted. Knowledge was becoming hard to find, and the same questions were being raised again and again. The network distilled and validated the content of the messages on a website, so members could look there first for frequently asked questions. This allowed the knowledge to be reused easily.

Enabling networks tend to be specialist in nature and are set up to fulfil a need when a core group is not co-located to sustain that discipline.

Enabling networks are encouraged to have a simple governing document, such as a terms of reference, for the benefit of the network, which includes aims and objectives, a statement of strategic value, and how it functions (see p. 132).

Being part of the community

So what does it feel like to be part of a network? When someone calls me to ask for some advice I feel valued and trusted. When I ask for help from others and get several timely responses I feel part of something larger than my immediate team. I enjoy the relationship I have with others in the community. People *Feeling valued* I encounter are passionate about what they are doing and *and trusted* what they know. I trust the know-how I get because I either know the person supplying it because I met them in a workshop last year, or I know someone else who knows them. I am confident that the person who made an offer will do what they said they would.

I have a sense that I have made real progress because I have achieved something in my work that I could not have achieved alone. And I have saved time doing it; time that I can use to do something else. In short, I feel a valued member of the community.

Knowledge management enabling network – terms of reference

The *aim* of the KM community is to deliver value to the business by increasing the effectiveness of KM practitioners around the group. The *objectives* of the KM community are:

- to realise value by embedding KM practice, process and behaviour in the business;

- to provide linkages and relationships between practitioners across the group thereby increasing effectiveness;

- to provide and maintain a mechanism so that people will seek and exchange operational knowledge about application of KM for business benefit; and

- to provide ownership, guardianship, and leadership concerning the principles of KM, as applied within the group.

Principles

The KM community will operate with a minimum of formality. It will be operationally focused, facilitated, and with membership by self-selection. Wherever possible, community members will be free and open with their questions and answers, sharing them through the community forum

Process

The KM community will be supported by:

- a membership list;

- a discussion forum linked to e-mail;

- a website representing the current state of knowledge of KM; and

- a facilitator who calls meetings, manages the discussion exchanges and maintains the website.

Members of networks tend to have peer recognition and are actively practising. They are good communicators and are active listeners. They are committed to improving the performance of the whole organisation, not just the performance of their immediate team.

Launching a community

Imagine you have identified some area of your business where knowledge is not evenly distributed. Let's say you work for an educational college, which is distributed on five campuses five miles apart. You know the people at the other campuses slightly because you have met some of them in occasional meetings. It's coming round to that time of year when the college needs to enrol students on the courses the college is offering.

Jill is in charge of enrolment. The college has clear targets for enrolment. After all, it needs to get the fees in to pay staff and cover operational costs. Jill calls a one-day meeting. Everyone with an interest in enrolment attends, including those who administer the enrolment, the curriculum managers, a representative from each subject area, and the marketing team.

In planning the meeting Jill considers the following:

1. How well do people know one another?

2. How established are the existing processes, language and good practices?

3. Are people comfortable working on shared documents from different locations?

She decides to focus on basic issues, such as target numbers, number of courses offered, which campuses will offer the courses. This focus will show quick results and create momentum. She allows for breaks in the meeting so people can make many connections that will be sustainable at a distance. She focuses on collaborative problem-solving rather than sharing good practice. She finds this gets more involvement and shares good practice as a by-product (see the structure of peer assists in Chapter 6, p. 57).

Coordinator's notes:
- *A rule of thumb is to meet face to face at least once a year to establish and maintain relationships. Communication can be maintained electronically but the relationship gradually decays. Meeting refreshes the relationship.*

- *Allow plenty of time for socialising in these gatherings. Avoid cramming the agenda.*

- *Sharing and collaborating with someone you know is much easier. Distributed communities depend on a core group meeting face-to-face at least once a year and are in regular contact.*

The meeting participants agree the key tasks to be completed within the timeframe and who will do what. Once the workshop is over, Jill sets up a rhythm of weekly phone conferences, and a discussion forum via an e-mail distribution list, to continue the dialogue started at the meeting. She nominates someone to coordinate the collection and sharing of all the information. Throughout the year people feel able to pick up the phone to people at other campuses to ask for help. They know who to talk to.

Coordinator's notes:
- *Provide a website and shared documents, such as contact details of members. This is invaluable to provide a sense of community.*

- *Shared artefacts (that is standards, principles we stand by, a common model, procedures) play a key role. The process of creating them, and the conversations that take place to agree them, are more important than the artefacts themselves.*

- *Introduce systematic learning into network processes, that is learning before, during and after.*

Everyone is clear about the enrolment process and the part they contribute. They feel good about their successful enrolment programme. The following year they meet again, already knowing one another and build upon the processes. They prove to be faster to implement and more effective.

Networks are mainly self-sustaining but they can benefit from some help and resources. Initially BP had a central knowledge management team. As part of its role, it encouraged the development and improvement of networks. It provided guidance and resources when needed, helped communities connect their agenda to business strategies. The KM team encouraged and challenged the networks, making sure the right people were included, and helped with links to other, similar networks.

Sustaining the network

The best networks in BP have someone coordinating the process, a single point of accountability energising the community when inactive and administering their shared information. It is important that the *network coordinator* is respected by the network, and is knowledgeable about the discipline, though preferably not the expert. The role is about helping others share what they know – the facilitator of the networking process rather than the fount of all knowledge. Coordinators given the position by management are sometimes regarded with suspicion. It is better if the network members select the coordinator and he or she clearly operates on behalf of the network members.

A coordinator helps others share rather than be the expert

Coordinators notes:

- *Establish a terms of reference, or a set of objectives with an internal customer.*

- *Communicate the results and celebrate successes.*

- *Identify and refresh membership, people leave and join according to their changing needs. Send personal welcome notes to new members.*

- *Ensure knowledge is captured, distilled, validated, shared and applied to improve business results.*

- *Ensure lively dialogue via discussion forums by identifying people to answer unanswered questions, cross-pollinating discussion threads, and finishing responses with questions.*

The network coordinator may have the role full time or combine it with his or her existing work. Whichever option, ensure your organisation recognises it is a legitimate activity, a key contribution to the effectiveness of the company.

Members

In a large organisation it is quite likely that not all the members will know each other. We use our Connect pages (see previous chapter) to make others aware of who the members are. We can list all of the members, send them an e-mail and even look at all of their photos, since it is often easier to remember a face than a name.

Recognition comes from peers and improved business performance

We are sometimes asked about reward and recognition for network members. Does BP give financial rewards for sharing knowledge? The answer is no. At BP, staff are encouraged to network when it makes sense to help business delivery. Network coordinators have their contribution explicitly reviewed as part of their annual appraisal.

The reward for sharing comes from peer recognition. Those who share believe it is a powerful mechanism to improve business performance – which *is* rewarded.

Committed leadership

Delivery networks thrive on support from senior management, to enable network activity to cross organisational boundaries. A model that works within our organisation has the network supported by both a sponsor and a mentor to provide a good framework 'like a three legged stool'.

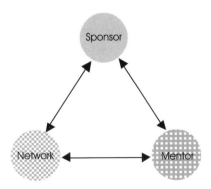

The sponsor, who is a key user of the network's output, brings a business focus, agrees a set of objectives with the Network coordinator and lobbies for resources where necessary.

Have a business sponsor act as customer ...

The mentor, usually head of a particular function or discipline, provides assurance of network performance to the sponsor, and coaching or resources to the network.

Network members are given the time to participate in network activities, and allowed to operate in an environment in which the value communities bring is acknowledged.

... and a mentor to coach and support

Tools for collaboration

Most networking occurs as a one-to-one interaction. Where the individuals are not co-located then they use a variety of collaboration tools to overcome the separation. The simple tools are the telephone and e-mail. Increasingly, people use video conferencing, and collaboration tools such as NetMeeting, to work together on a document or diagram simultaneously. If, like BP, you have people working in different time zones, then provide a shared space, and sufficient time to give people chance to contribute to the document.

Consider how you might work on a document with someone rather than create a draft for comment.

Communities as the guardians of the company's knowledge

Where does the knowledge reside in your organisation? We've talked about knowledge being in knowledge stores – as electronic and paper documents and maybe as audio and videotapes. Far more of it is in the heads of people working in the organisation. Networks are the best way we have found to access, maintain and refresh knowledge. They are key in validating and distilling know-how in their practice area. Knowledge does not remain static. It's not a case of storing a document on a shelf and leaving it to gather dust. The community has a role to play in adding to it, using it, deleting it when appropriate, distilling it and building it into business processes. Through sharing ideas, tips and hints, problems and solutions, they are able to access the knowledge of the whole community so that each individual can operate more effectively.

The community keeps the knowledge alive

No one is indispensable. This will be true only if the network shares its knowledge so no one person holds unique knowledge. Many of our networks build web pages, which hold the latest view of the knowledge of that practice area. We have a multitude of good-practice databases. Today those web pages and those databases 'die' when the owner moves. If the community, rather than the individual, assumes guardianship of the codified knowledge then it saves the company's knowledge from dependency on an individual.

See Chapter 11 (p. 141), on capturing knowledge, for more insights on this topic.

In this chapter we have explored why people are prepared to find the time to help others. We've looked at communities for spreading the company's knowledge more evenly. We have discussed what it takes to launch and to sustain these communities and finally we've examined their role as guardians of the company's knowledge.

We believe networks are essential in a flat organisation to share the company's know-how widely. The most effective networks within BP share the following characteristics:

Characteristics of effective networks

- Are empowered, are proactive, add value, and save time.

- Meet physically to develop rapport amongst the members.

- Have clear enabling mechanisms to sustain the interactions, methods such as intranet community pages, electronic discussion forums and shared tools and artefacts.

- Are clear whether they are developing the capability and competency of the organisation or whether they are focused on delivering something with *measurable* value.

- Have a clear, simple governing document, either a performance contract for a delivery network or a terms of reference for an enabling network.

- Elect a coordinator who manages the network processes and creates a rhythm of interactions.

- Have a sponsor who makes clear what the business needs, supports by finding resources and who speaks powerfully about the intent of the network.

Why not find out what it feels like to be part of a virtual community of practice? Join your fellow readers at: http://www.learning-to-fly.org

LEVERAGING WHAT WE'VE LEARNED – CAPTURING KNOWLEDGE

In this chapter:

- Why it is important to capture knowledge.

- How to make captured knowledge accessible through 'knowledge assets'.

- How to capturing an event or key meeting in a way that involves everybody.

- How to capture knowledge from someone leaving their current role.

Professor John Henderson from Boston University once told a powerful story about the US Army to a gathering of senior BP managers. Before he started the story, he asked whether BP had any formal approach to capturing strategic knowledge. The chief engineer raised his hand and described a database of 'project lessons learned'. John acknowledged this, and went on to tell this story:

A powerful story from the US Army

'I interviewed a colonel. Now this colonel was a colonel in one of the more elite groups in the US Army. He got a call on Saturday morning at 8 o'clock reminding him that a hurricane had just hit. He was told that because the current administration had very

strong ties to that particular part of the country that they did not believe that this should be left to the reserve group because they wanted "no screw-ups".

'*So the orders to the colonel were very clear: go down there, provide any support necessary to the people after this hurricane and don't screw up. Clear orders. The army calls it intent – strategic intent. The strategic intent was clear.*

'*This particular colonel had never actually commanded any type of civilian-related activity. He'd always been right on the front lines in hot action. It turns out as part of the executive education in the army, he had been exposed to the "Centre for Army Lessons Learned" as part of their executive education process.*

'*So he got on his laptop computer he dialed into Army net, hooked into the Centre for Army Lessons Learned and asked the following question – he actually showed me the type:*

```
"What does the Army know about hurricane
clean-up?"
```

'*Within four hours he had:*

- *A profile of the deployment of troops in the last three hurricanes that occurred in North America that the army was sent to provide support and clean-up including types of staff, types of skills, numbers of skills.*

- *He had a pro-forma budget – both what budget was required and what the actual budget was and where the cost overruns were.*

- *He had the ten questions that you will be asked by CNN in the first 30 minutes on your arrival.*

- *He had a list of every state agency and federal agency that had to be contacted and coordinated with and the name of the person that he had to contact with, and the army liaison person who was currently working with that group some place in North America.*

- *And he had established an advisory team of the three commanders, who agreed to be his advisory group in this command structure, four hours later.*

Then John Henderson asked: 'Is this of relevance to British Petroleum?' A pregnant pause followed, after which the chief engineer again raised his hand.

'You asked whether we had a formal approach to capturing knowledge? Well, we have nothing, *nothing* at all that is anything like *that*!'

Why capture knowledge in the first place?

Many people hold the view that the moment that something becomes codified – written down, physically or electronically – at that moment it becomes mere information and consequently loses value. True 'knowledge' is bound up in the context of the person telling the story, and you can't separate one from the other ...

In his book *Silent Messages*, Albert Mehrabian suggests that in any communication, roughly 7 per cent of the message is in the words, 38 per cent is in the tone of the voice, and the remaining 55 per cent of the message is communicated in body language. If this suggestion bears out, then we lose 93 per cent of the message – the context – when we reduce someone telling a story to a simple textual document.

Loss of context when capturing knowledge as information

In an ideal world, we would all share knowledge in a face-to-face, and never need to capture anything. The only difficulty here is none of us is omnipresent! We can't all be everywhere at once, so what's needed is a way to represent knowledge in a way that makes sense to others without losing too much of that context.

The challenge to learn, and the practical challenge of 'when to stop'...

But even that's not enough, how many stories are you prepared to read before you feel that you've learned enough? Five? Ten? Or just one or two that seem to justify what you've already planned to do?

That's the trouble. We struggle to absorb all the information available to us, and yet still don't feel knowledgeable.

These days everyone complains about information overload, but you never hear anyone complaining about 'knowledge overload'.

Tell me the ten things I need to know

In BP, the heartfelt plea of many people has been 'I don't have time to read all these reports – just tell me the ten things that I really need to know.'

So there's the challenge: we need to capture knowledge in a way that retains as much context as possible so that we can multiply its benefit. We also need to distil the key learning themes whilst avoiding the generation of a set of 'motherhood and apple pie' statements, so that people quickly find their way to the most relevant points.

Think back to the US Army hurricane example. What was it that was so powerful about John's story? Everyone could identify with the colonel being set a task that he didn't know how accomplish. What were the elements that we could learn from, and bring into, our own environment?

- Actual documents and plans used in previous hurricane clean-up exercises.

- Access to exactly the right detail of information where it was needed – the actual and planned budgets for each previous event, and the profile of troops deployed.

- Access to people – to precisely the right people with a commitment to help him as a virtual advisory team.

- Access to summarised, critical points – such as the first ten questions that CNN might ask – something the colonel might not have known to ask for.

- All within four hours of asking one simple question.

On the basis of that story, BP's knowledge management team worked to create a framework for capturing knowledge that incorporated these principles – we gave that framework the name 'knowledge asset', and set about learning how to create and sustain them inside the company.

Much of what we do is repeated in one way or another. We build petrol stations in Venezuela, then Japan, then Poland. Each of these actions generates its own story – its own record of what happened, what the context was, what lessons were learned. After a short time, this library of stories begins to build. Staff in Japan read what happened in Venezuela, put that experience to work locally, and create their own story.

Repeatable processes should eliminate repeatable mistakes

Over time, the volume of reading material could increase dramatically, much as people like reading stories, there are practical limits. This is where the value of *distillation* comes through. Consistent patterns begin to emerge that are common across the stories – Venezuela, Japan, Poland – these patterns then form the basis of a set of key guidelines as part of a knowledge asset.

Distillation makes knowledge more accessible

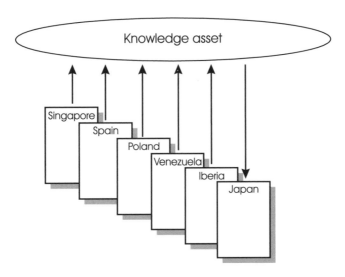

BP is a global energy company, and a large part of our business comes from the discovery and processing of crude oil.

Some crudes are tar-like in their consistency, others are far less viscous – in all cases, the oil itself is a tremendously complex cocktail of components. No two crudes are ever chemically the same, but most of them smell unpleasant!

We employ some very smart people who have the skills and the technology to analyse samples of crude oil and then characterise their properties – each one having a unique 'fingerprint' that indicates the likely constituents into which it might be separated. Crude Oil Assay – the technical term for this work – is a highly-skilled job, done by just a few people.

However, we don't create useful products from crude oil by analysis – we distil it on an enormous scale, into its commercially viable components, at refineries. Large fractionating columns subject the oil to the right combination of pressure and temperature, and the simple, refined products are distilled off at various points – refinery gas, LPG, gasoline, heavy fuel oil, and so on. Anyone working at that part of the refinery could point out to you the product extracted at that stage – whether it went in your car engine, or the fuel tank.

Let's move on from the distillation of crude oil and think about the analogy for capturing and packaging knowledge.

Whilst the laboratory expert could characterise and accurately describe the components of a crude oil sample, it didn't really have utility until the component parts were separated and made accessible by the process of distillation. At that point, the value can be realised, and these components can become the basis of other commercial products.

Think about day-to-day business in your organisation. Somewhere in the complex mixture of experiences, relationships, conversations and documents lie some simple powerful insights – insights

Distil the insights

which have commercial value and should be made easily accessible to others. So the trick is to take that mixture and distil it into a reusable set of lessons which can be accessed and explored by others in the organisation. Lessons which instantly answer the question 'What are the first ten things which I need to know?'

Here are the ten steps for creating a knowledge asset that have been tried and tested in some of BP's most critical knowledge areas.

Guidelines for building a knowledge asset

1. Is there a customer for this knowledge?

Have a clear customer – current or future – in mind when considering the creation of a knowledge asset. Without a customer, you may be creating a 'knowledge graveyard'. Who has, or will have a need to know something? Even if the requirement for this knowledge is not immediate, think about the needs of a *potential* future customer.

Ten steps towards creating a knowledge asset

For example, perhaps have the opportunity to gather insights from a series of mergers or acquisitions. Even if the next merger is months or years away, put yourself in the place of the person leading such an activity. What would make this knowledge asset invaluable to that person?

2. Are you clear what your knowledge asset is really about?

What is the scope of your knowledge asset? What will it be called?

A knowledge asset needs to cover a specific, and not too broad, area of business activity.

Examples of knowledge assets in BP include:

- conducting a turnaround at a refinery;

- transferring ownership of an offshore platform; and

- restructuring and right-sizing our business.

Which topics would be most valuable to your organisation?

You need to get some idea of what the content of this knowledge asset will be. Try this. Ask yourself:

- 'What do I need to know in order to do business?'

- 'What is the biggest issue facing me today?'

- 'Do I need to know processes, techniques, people, reasons for acting?'

- 'Do I need know-who, know-what and know-why in addition to know-how?'

- 'Why bother? What difference would it will make if I didn't capture this knowledge?'

3. Is there a community of practice relating to this subject?

Knowledge assets should be owned by communities of practice, who regularly refresh the content to keep it current. The community will be the source of the knowledge in the first place, the users of the knowledge in future, and the people who validate the knowledge in the knowledge asset. For example, the asset 'how to drill effectively in deep water' is owned by the drilling engineers. If there is no existing community of practice, you should establish one, if appropriate – in fact, the very process of collating history and exchanging knowledge may be a powerful catalyst in bringing the community together.

Communities of practice are the guardians of knowledge assets

4. Is there existing material upon which you can base your knowledge asset?

Gather what's already there

Often, someone in the company will have made efforts to record lessons or recommendations in some form – this will be important content to incorporate into your knowledge asset. Your first step will be to collate the existing material.

This may include:

- lessons learnt reports and project completion reports;

- the results of any After Action Reviews or retrospects;

- interviews with key players; and

- researching important documents and artefacts, such as project plans, communications plans, sample presentations and project processes.

If you are working in a new area, you may need to conduct interviews and introduce some learning processes such as After Action Reviews and retrospects, in order to generate the content for the knowledge asset. Additionally you could consider the wealth of information that exists beyond your company's walls, either from the Internet, or other external sources.

OK, you're half way there. Make yourself a generous cup of coffee, take a deep breath, lock the door and immerse yourself in the content.

5.   Look for the general guidelines

Provide some context so that people can understand the purpose and relevance of the knowledge asset. What was the business environment when this was created? Why was this seen as important at the time? Who brought this material together?

A knowledge asset works as a general guide for future use in all contexts. Go through the historical records of previous work and extract the knowledge from the context in which it sits. Different people will have seen certain approaches work at certain times.

Are there general guidelines that you can distil out of this material?

Provide a distillation of the key messages

The distillation is a creative and value-adding step – probably the most important one. You are taking what may be a mass of material, and distilling it out into something really useful. It doesn't have to be a solo effort, but it is not something that you would engage a large group to try and do. In all cases, it will require a block of uninterrupted time (a day or more in most cases), space, your undivided attention, a pair of scissors and a set of coloured marker pens.

6. Build a checklist illustrated with examples and stories

The checklist should tell the user of the knowledge asset:

- 'What are the questions I need to ask myself?'

- 'What are the top ten things that I need to think about?'

- 'What is the information that I need to gather?'

- 'What are the steps that I need to take?'

Checklists, rule-books and question sets

How you present this checklist is entirely up to the customer. Some people seem to respond better to a set of questions (e.g. 'Have you considered using a facilitator?') rather than to a set of rules and procedures (e.g. 'Use a facilitator where appropriate'), whilst others will prefer to work to a 'rule book'.

Check with your community of practice which format people prefer, rather than risk distracting or irritating the readers.

Stories and quotes bring knowledge back to life

Checklists generally read as dry and academic, and it helps if you illustrate them with examples, stories, pictures, models, quotes, video and audio clips, if possible. Get agreement from the individuals referenced, and make sure that they are happy with sharing their quote or clip more widely.

Recycle your key documents

It can also be valuable to include links to important source documents, so the reader can follow things up further if they want or use them as a template. For example, BP's knowledge asset on 'Business Restructuring' includes project plans, communications strategies, presentation materials and briefing documents.

From the reader's perspective, they will usually access the knowledge assets via the checklist, and drill-down into the areas which interest them, through key quotes, as far as in-depth transcripts, video clips and these key documents.

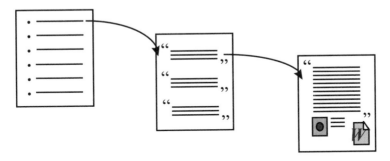

This book is an example of this structured approach. You can move from a high-level list in the table of contents, through to a more detailed description of each chapter, or into the chapter content itself.

7. Include links to people

Although the knowledge asset will include a lot of explicit knowledge, there will be far more knowledge still residing in the heads of the community of practice as tacit knowledge. This knowledge is also a vital part of the knowledge asset and it is important to point to it wherever possible. Create a hyperlink to the person's personal home page or e-mail address wherever you mention them in the text. Include a list of all the people with any relationship with the content – their photograph, e-mail address, telephone number and a link any personal home page (see Chapter 9, Finding the Right People). The photograph is significant, as it is psychologically much easier to contact someone if you know what they look like.

Point to people – the most valuable asset

Make sure you include your name and contact details (and photograph, if you like) at the bottom of the page. Additionally, provide details of the community of practice – who leads it, access to a discussion forum or mailing list.

8. Validate the guidelines

Validation comes from the community

You have now constructed a knowledge asset, with guidelines based on history and experience collected from the community of practice. The next step should be to circulate it around the community again, and ask, 'do the guidelines accurately reflect your knowledge and experience?', and 'do you have anything to add?'

9. Publish the knowledge asset.

You now need to make the explicit part of the knowledge asset widely available, so that the community of practice can access it at any time.

Select the right medium for publishing knowledge

Where you put it will depend on the nature of this community. The knowledge asset has to 'live with its owners'. For a local community this might be something as simple as an office wall, and for a global, or virtual community of practice, you will probably store the knowledge in virtual space – typically on the intranet. The power of the hyperlink means that original documents can reside with their owners, and just be linked-to from the knowledge asset.

Of course, you don't have to restrict yourself to a single medium. In the BP Norway office, the results of retrospects were put on the notice board by the coffee machines, where all the important managerial notices were posted. Everyone browsed this board daily, and the retrospect output was printed on bright coloured paper to catch the eye. The lessons were also sorted and put on the intranet, but posting them on the board was a key step in making them visible.

If the knowledge asset is a local one, serving a local community, then you could store it in physical space rather than electronically. An example of this would be the 'war room' that BP Vietnam set up as part of their knowledge management program. This was a room where people could gather before and after negotiations with the government, where they could hold After Action Reviews (AARs) and share what they knew. It held a large chart on the wall that was updated after every meeting, and a filing cabinet in the corner containing the records of all the AARs.

10. Finally, keep it alive. Initiate a feedback and ownership process

When you publish the knowledge asset, make sure there is a visible feedback mechanism so that users can validate through use. You will want to encourage feedback from users, so that they pick up and eliminate any invalid recommendations, and suggest new material. Make sure there is some sort of maintenance mechanism. Instil a sense of obligation that 'if you use it, then you should add to it'. Responsibility for maintenance may lie with the facilitator for the community (network leader or similar). Alternatively, this responsibility can move from one business unit to another as activity migrates within the business.

For example, the knowledge asset for deep-water drilling was created initially by the Gulf of Mexico business unit, then used by Scottish Foinaven field, updated by them then used by its neighbour, Schiehallion. Similarly, it could make sense if the refinery currently running a turnaround took ownership of the 'turnarounds' knowledge, making sure it was complete before, and updated after, the exercise.

In a way, it's a little like carrying the Olympic torch – keeping the flame burning for the next team.

One way of reinforcing the link between the knowledge asset, and the actual business events, is to include a 'news' section on the website, where you can list future events. The 'Refinery Turnarounds' knowledge asset does exactly this, listing a timetable of future turnarounds for refineries around with world. This builds awareness in the community of practice, and increases the likelihood that the content will be used at the time when it most useful.

Ownership of a knowledge asset can be transferred – like the Olympic flame!

There's a danger that this all sounds like a simple recipe – one that can be guaranteed to create the perfect result every time.

The reality is that sustaining a knowledge asset is more difficult than creating it in the first place.

Our experience is that success hinges on the active presence of a community of practice who feel a strong sense of ownership for the content. Without that, the result can be

Sustaining a knowledge assets is the toughest part

an elegant website ... that rapidly falls into disrepair and becomes a monument to some fine research. Alternatively, an individual takes editorial charge of the knowledge asset, and religiously maintains it, but fails to take into consideration the opinions of the rest of the community.

Unfortunately, it's easier to create a company expert than to sustain a company-wide community.

The result in this case can be a testimony to that individual's expert opinion, rather than the shared view of a group of people who act collectively as stewards of the company's intellectual capital. This is the difference between one person declaring what they do as 'good practice', rather than good practice being acclaimed by a group of people.

Moving towards good practices

Initially, what gets captured in knowledge assets are *practices* – success-ful ways of working that are applied somewhere inside the organisa-tion. Sometimes these are applied by other businesses and can be called *common practices*. Occasionally, *good practices* emerge from these common practices, as adoption 'snowballs' and a community of practice validates and recommends a practice.

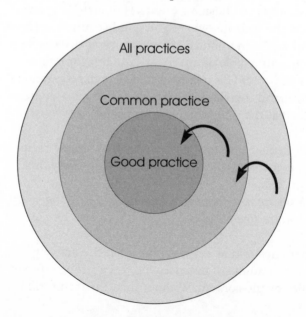

The ease with which good practices emerge is a reflection of the culture in the organisation. Where a 'not invented here' culture is prevalent, practices remain in the 'outer ring', as each business defends its own way of operating, rather than learning from others.

Where staff are encouraged to seek out knowledge, whether in knowledge assets or in the heads of other individuals, then good practices are more likely to emerge. The existence of a knowledge asset will raise awareness of what practices exist, and the presence of community of practice serves to accelerate the process of validation and widespread adoption of good practices.

Communities identify good practices

Capturing the essence of a key event

This story you are about to read is now a few years old, yet the principles are still completely relevant today. *How do you capture the essence of a significant event, so that people who didn't attend in person can feel as though they participated?*

For your organisation, perhaps, this might be a product launch, a shareholder meeting or an annual general meeting?

In late 1997, BP held an internal meeting (known as a colloquium) on the subject of innovation. It was a major meeting, and involved bringing together over 70 of the company's top management with experts from outside our industry for two intensive days.

Creating a management event for the whole organisation, then capturing it for the future organisation

In order to make the meeting more accessible to the rest of the company, it was decided that, in addition to the VHS video of the presenters, a 'live' website would be created for the event. The intent was twofold:

- to demonstrate openness by enabling the entire company to participate and contribute; and

- to capture a vivid and engaging record of the event for future reference.

The website was created, and a team posted an extract of each session onto the website approximately every two hours. The extract included photographs, sound bites, transcripts of key quotes, and a journalistic summary of the discussion or presentation in question, headlined by a catchy or provocative title.

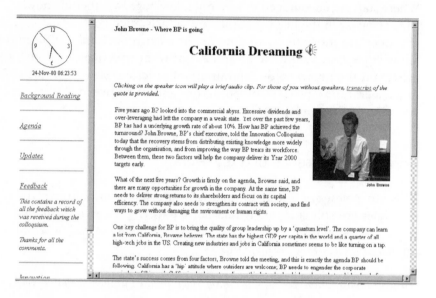

Additionally, feedback, ideas and challenges from the entire company was solicited via e-mail, and a summary of 'what the company is saying' was brought into the room and worked by the senior managers present. It was a truly inclusive process.

In today's world, where entire rock concerts are regularly webcasted to a potential audience of millions via the Internet, this all sounds rather low-key. Yet somehow, the product was more powerful because it wasn't as complete as a video stream of the event. Like a knowledge asset, the added value came through the accessibility and extraction of key points. Interestingly, three years later, the website is still accessed – dipped into for key quotes and summaries, whereas the VHS videos have been all but discarded. We felt that we had discovered something powerful in having a near real-time abridged summary of the event, complete with photographs, audio-clips and a simple process for anyone, anywhere in the company to participate in the discussion.

The retrospect

Needless to say, we conducted a retrospect with the team. Here are some excerpts.

What we set out to achieve
An innovative process and product to support the colloquium, using the web to involve more that just the delegates. The context was for the colloquium not to be seen as exclusive, and the idea was to use the intranet to allow a degree of virtual participation.

Learning after the event. Lessons on how to capture a management event

What did happen?
All objectives were achieved or exceeded. Virtual participation was greater than expected, and a lot of positive feedback has been received. People who joined the colloquium virtually were pleased that their feedback was noticed. The sponsor was delighted. The website was 'hit' by 4000 different people during the three days of the colloquium.

Lessons learned
- A multidisciplinary team is a success factor. We had the freedom to choose people who were professionals in their own right, rather than trying ourselves to do the specialist roles. Ideal team roles would be:

  - A journalist, to produce brief exciting, headlined summaries in real time. This is crucial.
  - A web designer/developer.
  - Someone responsible for monitoring feedback from website users.
  - Someone receiving onto his or her PC a live video stream, who can identify and extract the video and audio-bytes.
  - An editor for the text content (this person should be BP staff if the event is high profile).
  - A team leader responsible for: project management, content editor for the website, summarising (and presenting) feedback.

- A live website forms a support for a major event, focused towards the outside world, but can also provide feedback to the event from the rest of BP. This feedback from collective BP needs to be introduced into the forum by somebody giving summaries.

These summaries themselves need to be captured and put on the web, to demonstrate the effectiveness of the process. The fact that one of the presenters included quotes from the feedback was proof of the effectiveness.

- Any feedback should go straight onto the site with no filtering or editing – just as if the person was there in the room.

- Workload is very 'peaky'; the editor does all the checking and approvals when the room goes out for a break. Be especially sensitive to his/her needs.

What the customers said

The feedback from the virtual participants was tremendous:

'I have just spent an hour going through the Colloquium website and have a real sense of "having been there" and being energised by the content.

What the participants said ...

'That is a real achievement and makes this effort very distinct from the normal, dry, paper output. The speed of the delivery of the material, its immediacy (pictures and audio clips) and its relevance is quite extraordinary. You should be extremely well pleased with this piece of innovation.'

Business unit leader in Norway

'Greetings to you all from Thistle A – a very mature asset in the Northern North Sea. We are all avid readers of the site and think it is an excellent idea – innovation itself! We look forward to visiting the site over the next few days and we thank you for the opportunity to give input. Team Thistle'

Collective contribution from the crew of an oil rig in the North Sea

'This is a great example of innovation, encompassing people, process and technology! It is enabling people way beyond the walls of Durdent Court to feel able to participate. I'm accessing this today in Anchorage and next week I'll be dipping in from deep in the Sahara Desert. This is sharing what we know and learn on a grand scale!'

Business consultant in Alaska

'The live Innovation Colloquium website has been for us a great success. 'The quality and breadth of feedback made a real contribution to the Colloquium, stimulating our thoughts and providing us with great encouragement. This experiment has revealed a powerful new tool we can use to help us draw widely on ideas and experience from across the company as we do so. Thanks to all who contributed.'

The managing director who sponsored and attended the event

In the three years that have passed since the Innovation Colloquium, information technology has advanced, and many variations and adaptations of this approach have been tried and tested in BP.

Several workshops and events have been recorded onto CD-ROM, and distributed to a wider audience. This medium enables far greater use of video than the company intranet would support, in effect converting each event into an electronic learning tool.

Typically, such tools would include:

- a simple, easily navigable index of the event;

- succinct video clips of speakers synchronised with their presentation material – often PowerPoint slides;

- longer videos to add further depth to the succinct sound bites if the reader requires it;

- full, searchable transcript of everything that was said;

- copies of all the presentation materials used;

- videos of the attendees expressing their impressions of the event; and

- contact information for all the attendees.

Webcasting a technical presentation for the specialists ...

Additionally, webcasting technology has been used to transfer BP's technical expertise around the globe. In one recent example, drilling experts from the Wytch Farm oilfield in Dorset, southern England participated in an interactive broadcast over the intranet with staff in Aberdeen, London and Houston. The webcast took the form of a presentation, synchronised with a live video window of the engineers in Dorset. The participants could interact with the slides, and actually rotate and zoom in on images of the drilling technology in question. Additionally, a live chat room enabled the participants to ask questions of the presenters or each other, creating a virtual classroom across the company.

Whilst the live presentation was powerful and interactive, the process of webcasting created a permanent record of the event that can be accessed at any time.

... and a corporate presentation for the generalist

On 11 July 2000, three of BP's directors gave a presentation on BP's financial performance and strategy to the financial analysts' community. The presentation was simultaneously webcast inside the company direct to the desktops of thousands of employees, enabling them for the first time to receive the news at the same time as the analysts – as well as providing a complete record for those who missed the 'live event'.

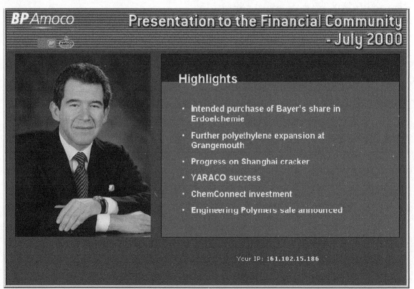

Whichever approach you chose to take, information technology unquestionably has a key role to play in making captured knowledge accessible.

However, more important is the ability to distil, reduce, focus, structure and headline the content in such a way that the readers can experience the full breadth of subject matter and quickly pinpoint what they are looking for. Technology can have seductive power, but content will always be king.

Capturing knowledge from someone leaving their position

Ideally, if knowledge management principles have been applied during the time an employee spends with the company, then much of that person's knowledge will have been captured over time in e-mails, discussion forums and knowledge assets. Knowledge capture and transfer is a natural outcome of all of the processes and tools referenced in this book, hence personal knowledge capture should not be the only record of an individual's contribution to the company.

If you're already managing knowledge routinely, then the personal loss is diminished

Here's an example of this.

When the majority of BP's knowledge management team left the company in 1999, a huge amount of their personal knowledge and experience was already embedded in a rich website (effectively a knowledge asset), an extensive discussion forum, and a community of several hundred enthusiasts remaining in the company. Writing this book would have been a far greater challenge without the commitment of the team to live their own principles.

However, we recognise that the real world doesn't always operate as smoothly as an elegant model …

Think about the last time that you moved on from a position. Did you capture anything for the person filling your role? Or think about when you started your current role. What questions would you have liked your predecessor to answer?

Retaining corporate memory when people move on

At times of significant business restructuring, many people will be leaving their jobs, either to move somewhere else in the organisation, or to leave the company completely. In day-to-day business, people move rapidly from one field to another unrelated position elsewhere in the company. Very often these people possess key knowledge – knowledge either about the business and their role, or about a discipline or function.

What about the 'what's in it for me' factor? Why should someone actually want to capture their personal knowledge?

Leavers who have had the opportunity to talk through their job, feel better about leaving (even if they are leaving the company involuntarily). They feel a sense of closure, and they feel a sense of professional satisfaction that they are leaving the post, or the community, in safe hands.

How can we retain knowledge when the people move on? It would be wonderful to say that we use these techniques with every member of staff leaving the company but the truth is that we're not particularly good at this. Where this approach to personal knowledge capture *has* been effective in BP, the following six steps illustrate what was done.

Please tell us if you know of instances where companies routinely do this – the authors would welcome any examples (see Resources 2, p. 215, for contact information).

Find a customer (or customers) for the knowledge.

Who needs to know what the leaver knows? In the case of a key business player, it may well be his/her successor who is the customer for the knowledge. It the leaver is a global expert, then the customer for the knowledge is a network, or someone acting on behalf of the network.

Facilitator's notes:
What if no successor has been identified yet? In this case it is perhaps even more important that someone takes responsibility for capturing the knowledge, so the successor can be briefed when he/she is appointed.

Six steps for successful knowledge capture

1. Find out what knowledge needs to be transferred

This is typically a balance of 'What does the customer want to know about?' and 'What knowledge does the leaver feel is crucial?'

> *Balancing what needs to be heard with what needs to be said*

There are two basic approaches to deciding what knowledge needs to be transferred.

Firstly you can ask the leaver to identify the key knowledge, and this is best done using a checklist of questions designed to make him or her think carefully about what they know.

Facilitator's notes:
The purpose of the checklist is to get at the things which the leaver does not necessarily realise they know – those bits of knowledge which are automatic or subconscious, but crucial to the job. At this stage the leaver is not trying to capture the knowledge itself, but to identify the priority areas. The second approach is to ask what knowledge the customer wants to gain.

Chris Dewey leads a network of 30 worldwide professionals concerned with knowledge about grease, and was planning to capture knowledge from a global expert in the subject of grease lubricants. She went out to the Grease network and asked them each for three questions they would like the expert to answer. Many of them came back and said that three was not enough – they had dozens of questions!

By asking for three, or five, or ten questions and comparing the knowledge needs of the customer and the 'knowledge offers' from the leaver, you can then build a list of prioritised knowledge areas that need to be transferred.

2. Develop a plan to capture and transfer the knowledge.

Now you know the key areas of knowledge which need to be retained when the leaver moves on. How do you most effectively capture it and transfer it?

The answer to this depends very much on whether it is a job handover, where someone will be filling the leaver's post. If this is the case, then the best plan is to set up a meeting or meetings between the leaver and his/her successor. You can then give the successor accountability for capturing all the knowledge they think they might need. In certain circumstances, where there are other customers for the knowledge in addition to the successor, you might like to include some of these people in the meeting.

If there is no clear successor, or (as in the case of a global expert leaving) the knowledge is needed by a whole community of people, then alternative approaches are needed.

Although the leaver could try to capture all the knowledge himself, it is better to do it with a facilitator, or an interviewer, or (best of all) a representative of the network or community.

3. Conduct the interview

It's a good idea to go through the knowledge transfer meetings using some sort of checklist or structure, so that all areas of knowledge transfer are covered.

Not just know-how – but know-what, know-why and know-who as well!

Rather than just concentrating on 'know-how', consider 'know-who', 'know-what', and 'know-why'. Use prompts to jog the leaver's memory, as described below. Tape-record, or even video the meeting so that you can produce a transcript, and some useful sound bites. This will be a very rich experience, and you may not get a second chance.

Facilitator's notes:
Remember, this is intended to be a mutually beneficial conversation rather than an audit or inquisition. Be sensitive at all times to what the leaver is comfortable discussing.

4. Now make it accessible

If the knowledge only needs to pass from the leaver to the successor, then you don't need to do much 'packaging'. The successor can keep it all on file somewhere, or in written notes and transcripts. If the knowledge needs to go to a network, or community of practice, then more effort is needed. This knowledge will need to be made accessible and searchable to the whole network, which probably means putting it on the intranet. Some of the ideas you could consider are as follows:

- Writing a frequently asked questions (FAQ) based on the questions from the network and the expert's answers, and make it widely available.

- Using the expert's presentations, plus his recorded comments on each slide, as a teaching aid.

- Copying the title page of each of his/her books, and recording a paragraph of his comments on each one.

- Recording video summaries of key issues.

- Summarising his/her key stories, to act as company history.

- Summarising his/her recommendations, illustrated by key quotes, to act as the basis for a knowledge asset.

- Creating a 'relationship map' of key contacts, complete with photographs.

What you should have at this stage is a set of captured knowledge (in the form of notes, a website, video, or transcribed tapes), a successor or customer group who feel they have been briefed, and a happy leaver with a sense that they are valued.

5. Stay in touch

Aim to stay in touch with the leaver if you can. No knowledge transfer or capture will ever be 100 per cent, and there will come a time when you think of that key question you wish you had asked. Make sure you can contact the leaver in future so you can tap his/her experience again. Your company may have invested heavily in developing this individual – you will know of their professional quality and they will know about the company culture. You may want to bring them back on a consultancy

Don't cut the cords unless you have to

basis in the future. BP's yellow pages directory (see Chapter 9, Finding the Right People), 'Connect' includes the capacity for staff leaving the company to leave their details 'in the system' after they have left the company, if they choose to.

6. Summary

We have now considered three approaches to capturing knowledge – consolidating a set of stories into a community-owned knowledge asset, capturing an event, and retaining corporate memory by interviewing a member of staff about to leave their current role. Knowledge capture in any form takes time and effort, but the potential yield to BP has been high – millions of dollars in some cases, so the time and effort is well spent.

So we've now learned before, during and after, we know who knows, we've shown what is known by the community and we've even captured it. Just how can we put it all together?

Part

Today and Tomorrow

3

EMBEDDING IT
IN THE ORGANISATION
– PREPARING TO LET GO

In the previous chapters we have shared the tools and methods that we have applied within BP to practice knowledge management. This chapter presumes knowledge of the other chapters; so if you started here, skip back to the earlier chapters.

Where do we go next? What is the 'next wave' for knowledge management? This chapter is about how we are developing the capability in the organisation to manage knowledge without help from a central resource – allowing us to move on to the other challenges.

The chapter includes:

- Preparing to let go.

- The phases of KM activity.

- Working yourself out of a job.

- Focusing on a company-wide business process.

- Where next?

Learning to fly

Imagine an eagle encouraging its young to leave the nest. They huddle together in the nest, high up on a wild crag. When the mist lifts they can see forever. The parents have nurtured them, sheltered them from the wind and rain and protected them from prey. Now it is time for them to fly. There is no way for them to clamber down the cliff and practice at a lower level. So the mother pushes them out of the nest with her beak and watches after them.

Down, down, down they drop. Their wings come out to steady them. Still they drop. They continuously beat their wings. The ground is fast approaching. Slowly they glide over the treetops. They beat their wings some more. Without looking back they head across the lake shore looking for their first own-caught meal.

The mother catches up with them and demonstrates the art of catching a warm thermal current, to elevate themselves to a higher level. They glide along the face of the crags, looking graceful and powerful. In fact they look as if they have been flying forever.

In time they will mate and have offspring. They too will have to stand back and let others learn to fly.

We also have to learn to stand back and let others learn to do it for themselves. Based on our experience of applying knowledge management techniques we see some distinct stages in the relationship between a dedicated resource and the business teams that they work with.

Creating *awareness*. This involves a presentation and discussion about what knowledge management is and where it has been used to leverage business results. Examples of successful application are key to enrolling others. This is most powerful if peers speak about how they have applied knowledge management, and the difference that it has made to their business. A practical way we have found to do this, if the peer is in a different location, is to record and show a short video clip. The awareness stage is a two-way exchange. What is the biggest current issue or challenge for the business team?

Starting with something simple. Applying one of the tools and techniques in this book to address a simple part of the issue is a good start. Demonstrating a 'quick win' is important to gain the interest and commitment of the team. If they see that these techniques can be applied, without spending too much time on them, to deliver some tangible results, then they are likely to come back for more. We have found it best to introduce some formality after this stage into the planning. What specifically will be done, what are the costs and the benefits and will the team commit some resources to it?

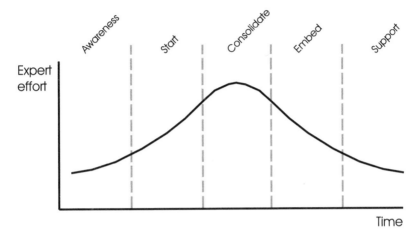

Consolidate. This builds on the simple beginning using the holistic model. Exactly what is done depends on the nature of the business challenge. It is likely the team will need some expert resource working directly with them, and at the same time they should encourage widening the number of people exposed to the processes.

Embed. At this stage the business team takes the lead and links what they are doing to their routine business processes. Meanwhile the experts take the role of advisors, and introduce new tools where appropriate.

Support. The experts have moved out from amongst the business team, but are available by telephone, e-mail and videoconference to encourage and support the efforts of the business. They also connect the business to others who could help or benefit from the learning.

In working through this sequence a number of times, we found that the toughest part is letting go. The business teams are busy and are grateful for the contribution from the experts. It takes the pressure off them, and they are helping deliver the business objectives. It creates a dependency relationship.

The toughest part is letting go

The experts feel good that they are needed. However, if the benefits are to be sustainable then the team must solve problems on their own. This will free the central resource to move on to the next task, building on what has been learned from this one.

In some ways I suppose it's the same as letting go of teenage children. My two have grown up. I am not quite sure when it happened. I used to make all the decisions for them, but now they have minds of their own. My son drives the family car late at night and we worry till he is back. My daughter goes out clubbing and catches a taxi back in the early hours. Will she be safe? We have shared our values and behaviours with our children for several years. They have watched what we do as much as what we say. We have instilled in them a capability to survive. Now they must take their own decisions. And we must learn to let go.

Learning to live without a central knowledge-management resource

So as a central knowledge management team we have instilled in the organisation the capability to share and apply know-how. The team has disbanded. Some have found new challenges within the company where they can make a significant difference. Others have left to consult externally. In either case, as external or internal consultants, success in embedding knowledge management in one project is the reference required for getting the next job.

Let's stop and reflect for a moment. Identify three areas of your business or department where you can make the biggest difference to performance. Then go back and look at the holistic model to use as a check. (see Chapter 3, p.27, The Holistic Model). Are you learning before, during and after? Do you have a way for routinely capturing and refreshing the knowledge gained? Who are the people are involved? Is there a community who feel accountable for looking after and sustaining this knowledge?

What is the 'next wave' for knowledge management?

BP is focusing on some key company-wide processes: health, safety and environmental (HSE) performance; capital productivity; and operational excellence. KM principles are being embedded in each of these so that they become the normal way of doing business. If we can take a good practice from one business and replicate it in several other places, just think of the potential value added. The aim is to improve collaboration, the role of networks as guardians of the company's knowledge, recognising and using the value of the company's knowledge and reducing the time to competency by linking knowledge assets to the learning programme. *These are the 'thermals' that will sustain the young bird in flight, and enable it to soar higher.*

Embedding knowledge management in core processes

Let's have a look at what is happening.

Knowledge management and HSE performance

Health, safety and environmental performance is a big-ticket item across the entire company. It is something that every employee is accountable for, and something that is actively promoted in all offices (remember those stickers on the mirrors in the earlier chapter?).

No harm to people or the environment

BP's policy on health, safety and the environment makes no mention of knowledge management. However it does explicitly reference *learning*:

> *How we learn from each other ...*

> *The HSE Toolbox will be maintained on the intranet containing good operating processes/practices, knowledge and audit protocols. These show good demonstrated practice from around the BP Group, and should be referenced when developing business management systems. More importantly, business personnel are encouraged to contribute their good practices to the HSE Toolbox in order to promote sharing and adoption of lessons learned.*

So how is knowledge management embedded into the HSE programme?

There is an HSE website that provides a focal point for all issues to do with health, safety and the environment. There is an assessment tool that enables different sites to check how their performance is and what they might do to improve. This is one area where every business is truly committed to improve so as not to harm people or the environment.

An intranet-based 'HSE Toolbox' is available to all staff, and provides details on good practices, assigned to the various HSE management processes. A network of staff take responsibility for each management process, and act as owners for the good practices in that area. This shared approach ensures a flow of new good practices, refreshing what is held in the toolbox. The whole process operates in a similar manner to the way we create and maintain knowledge assets (see Chapter 11 for more on capturing knowledge) – but we don't refer to knowledge assets anywhere – we simply call it a 'toolbox'.

Knowledge assets under a different guise

Whilst BP puts tremendous effort into avoiding health, safety or environmentally-related incidents, any incident or near miss is captured as part of a reporting system. The lessons learned from the incident are drawn out as part of the reporting process, and shared widely and rapidly across the organisation.

A network of HSE staff around the company are accountable for improving against their performance targets, and so maintain the knowledge and share it quickly around the organisation.

Knowledge management and projects

Company-wide, BP invests billions of dollars in projects each year: searching for new reserves of oil, accessing new markets for new products, building factories for the construction of solar cells, researching and developing cleaner fuels ...

Much management attention is devoted to improving the productivity of our capital projects, asking questions such as:

- How do we know that we are doing the *right* project?

- How do we know that we're doing the project *right*?

- What are the key risks associated with this project?

Are we doing the right projects?

- How does our return on investment compare with industry benchmarks?

Whether your projects have a budget of £10,000 or £100,000,000 you'll want to ensure that each project is managed in way that builds in the lessons and insights from other projects. But how can you create the impetus for learning, when project teams have a natural instinct to get into action?

BP's process for managing the life cycle of projects is known as the capital value process (CVP). It provides a framework for any project team, with a series of recognisable phases, and stage-gates that represent the decision points in moving ahead with the next stage of a project.

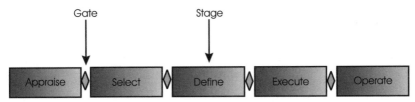

Capital value process – 5 stages

This process is used across the company, and has created a common language across project teams. When a team running a project to build retail sites in Poland talks with a team producing oil from the depths of the Gulf of Mexico, a common understanding that they are both working in

... and are we doing them right?

the 'define' stage of their respective projects will help them better understand each other's challenges.

So where does knowledge management find its way into this process?

For some time, a community of project-management professionals has been disciplined at holding post-project appraisals to capture the lessons from major projects. BP has been putting effort into energising this community, to get them acting as the guardians of the community's knowledge, and for refreshing and keeping the know-how alive. A distillation of these good practices is embedded in value improvement processes recognised by the projects community as a whole.

The CVP framework for managing projects includes some mandatory elements – things that a project team *must* do, in order to gain sanction for the next stage of a project. One of the necessary tasks to be completed for every stage is that the team hold a peer assist meeting (see Chapter 6 for more on peer assists), which gets creative input and options into their work, and a peer review, which is a way to get constructive challenge from other peer teams.

The impact of this simple, common process is very strong. Nobody can complete a project without learning from his or her peers on several occasions, and without seeking out which good practices can be applied from others.

Perhaps you are reading this thinking *'that's all very well, but we could never make such a rigorous process work in our company'*. Or perhaps *'our projects are much smaller scale, there is too much additional overhead in a process like this'*.

If embedding prompts for learning and knowledge-sharing in a process is not feasible, another option is to embed it in management behaviour by encouraging management to ask questions such as:

The power of a management team 'asking the right questions'

- Who has done this kind of thing before, that we can learn from?

- Who did you learn from before coming to me with this new idea?

- Who might benefit from knowing about what you've just achieved?

BP's Cooper River chemical factory in Texas did exactly this, and it quickly evolved into a low-key, but highly effective initiative they entitled 'borrowing and sharing'. A member of their administrative staff maintains a register of good practices that anyone at the factory has imported and applied (with measures of value where possible), or has been exported and applied by another business. Each year Cooper River's management team set an annual target for the number of good practices imported and exported (70 at the time of writing).

This simple act of *asking the right management questions* and keeping a register to raise the profile, has created a positive learning culture at the factory, which one of the workers referred to, in a tongue-in-cheek manner, as 'the lazy man's way to work'. That's certainly an interesting way to paraphrase 'knowledge management'!

Knowledge management as the lazy man's way to work!

And finally let's look at the role of knowledge management in the area of operations.

Knowledge management and operations excellence

We're going to spend a bit of time on this one, describing how we have put it all together. We are creating a community of practice across all of our operational businesses, providing tools, processes and encouraging the right behaviours to 'harness the knowledge of a thousand control rooms'.

BP has a flat organisational structure, around 150 businesses in what we describe as a 'federation of assets'. Each asset operates with a high degree of autonomy, functioning almost as a discrete company, highly focused on performance.

Encouraging sharing in a flat organisation

One risk that flat organisational structure carries is that the businesses operate independently, rather than interdependently. The operations excellence initiative was established to encourage sharing, not only between businesses of similar type (refineries, or manufacturing operations for example), but also across operations of different character. Underpinning this was a belief that the key principles of managing operations are actually common, regardless of whether the business is an offshore platform producing oil, or a factory producing polyethylene in Asia. Two thirds of our 150 business units are directly involved in operations of some description, hence there is high potential for sharing knowledge.

All of our operations people are working on issues relating to:

- management of people;

- safety and environmental performance;

- the ability to minimise unplanned down-time;

- effective project management;

- ensuring optimal production; and

- rigorous cost management.

So let's refer to the holistic model for a moment.

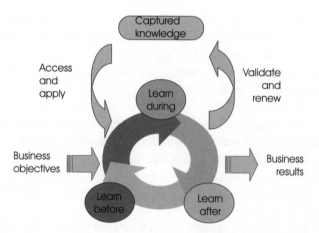

Check with the holistic model

Are we focused on delivering business results? Yes! So what are we doing to ensure learning before, during and after? What network is in place to facilitate the sharing? And what are we doing to continually capture the latest knowledge?

Common measures and a common assessment tool

Having recognised that our various operating businesses had more in common with each other than they might have thought, the next stage was to create a common language, a standard set of measures, and a single assessment tool which could be used universally to gauge performance and provide assurance for management.

A diverse team of operations staff representative of all our operating environments came together for several days. They included people who had worked on the HSE and CVP processes to ensure we were aware of, and used, the lessons from previous company-wide programmes. They worked to establish a common set of practices. These were the areas they felt were important enough to define

Creating a common language is a basis for sharing

and measure consistently. Additionally, these areas were inclusive – relevant across all aspects of the operations, whether producing oil from a reservoir, refining it, or manufacturing polymers.

Examples of these practices include raising morale and motivation, managing energy efficiency, forecasting production, and managing greenhouse gas emissions.

The full list of 26 practices is included as Appendix B, p. 203.

Having established these common areas of focus, drawing on expert help where necessary, the team designed a five-level assessment tool. This broke down each practice into several specific 'elements', and provided a set of five statements for each, ranging from a description of world-class performance (level 5) to a description of poor performance (level 1).

An example element (Reward and Recognition) from 'Raise Morale and Motivation' is given below:

Element: Reward and Recognition

Level 5: *all staff feel their contributions are valued, recognised and rewarded.*

Level 4: *most staff feel valued and appropriately recognised and rewarded as individuals and teams.*

Level 3: *a reward and recognition system in place but inconsistently applied.*

Level 2: *people see little connection between performance and reward.*

Level 1: *people feel victimised and blamed.*

Scoring of these levels is subjective, the key aim is to encourage a conversation to gain consensus on what an asset is good at and where they need to improve.

The assessment tool was rolled-out to all one hundred operating businesses to run for themselves as a self-assessment. Typically the operations manager would draw together a group of around ten people – a diagonal slice through their organisation – and the group would discuss and agree which of the statements was true from their perspective. This would provide an overall score for each practice – *'We are level three for managing greenhouse gases'* – for example.

Use a cross-section of people for a variety of perspectives

In addition to stating their current position, the team were encouraged to indicate which practices they planned to improve during the next two years, and by how much.

'We are currently level three for managing greenhouse gases, and have set a target of level five by end 2002' would be an example of this.

So that was it. Every operating business would work through the self-assessment and record two sets of scores – where they are today, and where they plan to be in two years time. We captured these scores via an intranet website. Having identified some gaps in their performance, the business would agree some specific targets relating to closing these gaps, and spend the remainder of the year actively working towards those targets. We summarised this as an improvement cycle, from measuring, to identifying gaps in performance, to planning and implementing actions, back to measuring improvements.

The operations excellence cycle

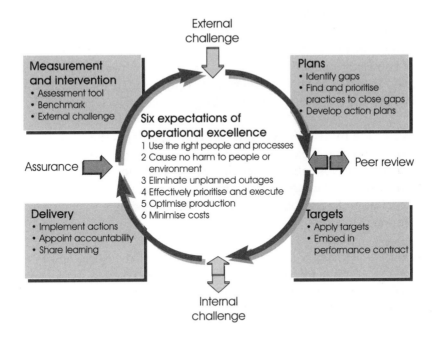

Providing the tools and resources that support improvement

Having a common set of practices enabled us to create a 'toolbox' (much like the earlier HSE example) of good practices, tips and techniques, each one allied to a particular practice. We built in a feature similar to one in Amazon.com that enables anyone to review an entry in the toolbox, and provide a 'star rating' from one to five. This democratic approach helped us to see which tools were truly useful.

The community maintains and refreshes its tools

Additionally, we worked to align a network with each of the practices, such that the network would become accountable for the range of tools and good practices available for that particular practice. In some cases this required us to merge several networks into one, whilst in others, a new network was encouraged to form.

In this way, the toolbox acted as a collection of knowledge assets that enable learning from what the company already knows, whether before, during or after an operational phase (see Chapter 11 for more on knowledge assets). BP's various operations networks became the custodians for each one, renewing and updating it and taking into account the star ratings provided by those actually using the tools.

One of the most effective ways of creating an appetite for learning was by offering a picture. A picture is worth a thousand words. A picture that illustrates at a glance how a company's operations are performing, is worth millions of dollars. A breakthrough in helping the organisation learn while doing was to devise a simple yet illustrative picture.

A common way of visualising performance Having a *common* set of assessment measures across all of our hundred business operations enabled us to create exactly that picture. The picture portrayed the range of scores against all of the practice areas that we had defined, and could be used as a backdrop against which any single business could measure itself. By referring to the picture the whole team could see the areas it performed well in, and areas where others were better. This is the first step towards asking for and receiving help.

Like the assessment matrix, the vertical axis was calibrated from level one (low performance) to five (world-class performance). The horizontal axis listed the various practices, side by side.

Having completed the self-assessment, any business could see its current performance scores laid out against this framework – a unique 'heartbeat trace' which represented their performance.

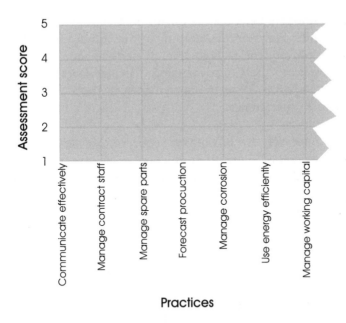

When their target scores were overlaid on this chart, the gaps between current performance and target performance became very clear, providing the managers of that business with some areas for focus.

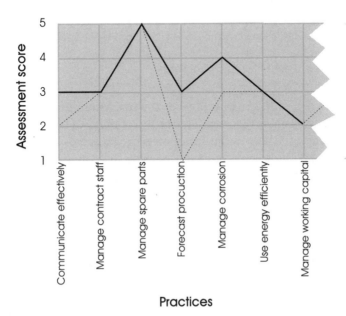

When we aggregated the scores for all businesses, we saw some common trends. For example, not one of our hundred operational businesses reported world-class (level 5) performance in the areas entitled 'Communicate Effectively' and 'Manage Greenhouse Gas Emissions'. This was of particular concern to those running our environmental programmes.

Plotting the scores and targets shows the gaps

Conversely, no businesses reported low performance in the areas of 'Forecast production' or 'Assure product quality'. We created a single picture that aggregated all the individual scores to illustrate these trends. We entitled the picture a 'river diagram'.

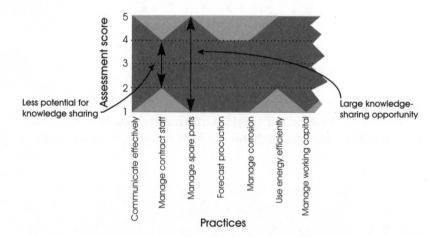

The boundaries of the river represent the maximum and minimum scores that any business reported. The 'banks' of the river are those areas mentioned earlier, where no businesses reported a score. The presence of a 'south bank' indicated competence inside the company (everyone at level 2 or above). The presence of a 'north bank' (no-one at level 5) pointed us towards external benchmarks rather than internal examples, as we lacked sufficiently high performance inside the company.

Where the river is widest you'll find opportunities for sharing

Finally, and most significantly from a knowledge perspective, the width of the river at any single point gave a clear indication of the potential for sharing and learning in BP. Where the river was narrow ('Manage contract staff', in the example above), most businesses were of similar performance, and no breakthroughs had been identified internally. Where the river was widest ('Manage spare parts', in this case) indicated a wide range of performance, hence tremendous opportunities for sharing and improving performance exist.

We were particularly interested in the wide points of the river because *suddenly, staring us in the face was a picture that showed us where to focus knowledge-sharing activities.* We encouraged and supported internal conferences, peer assists and the creation of knowledge assets on these topics.

The river diagrams proved to be a popular way to think about performance relative to the company as a whole. It would tell an operations manager how strong or weak their performance was relative to all others.

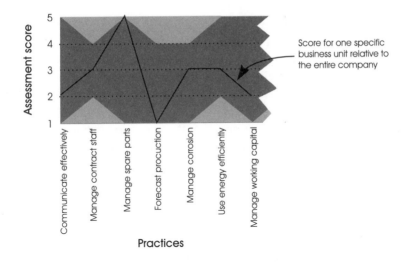

We have since used this diagram in other settings to good advantage. Take a few minutes to reflect on this. Is there an area of your organisation where if you identified a set of key practices, you could compare relative performance?

We created a process to encourage common measures and the sharing of good practices across all of BP's operational sites. Having a common language and a common self-assessment tool for all operations is tremendously powerful, and enables sharing between previously unrelated businesses. We also coached the senior management, to ask questions such as, 'who have you talked to in order to improve your operational performance?'

Because we had divided the assessment tool into practices, we measured the scores for each practice. We consciously declined to sum the scores across the practices to get an absolute score for a refinery or a chemical factory. We weren't interested in absolute comparison – we wanted to share the details on a practice-by-practice basis. Because *everybody* is good at *something*, there are always some positive messages for each business. At a recent BP operations conference, a senior manager stated:

> *'We have world class performance in almost every single practice – somewhere in the company. The trick is to recognise where it lies, and to apply it globally.'*

Additionally, we asked businesses to *set their own priorities* and record their own targets for improvement. For example, one of our chemical manufacturing plants in the US had a low score (1 out of 5, based on the assessment tool) for their ability to manage corrosion. Based on that data alone, you might anticipate that they have a local problem with corrosion. When that same factory recorded their target score (still 1 out of 5), it immediately becomes apparent that corrosion management isn't a business priority. The reality is that the factory in question makes a polymer product using a non-corrosive process, and experiences favourable weather conditions – corrosion simply isn't a big issue for them.

Unlike a project, this process is a continuous cycle of improvement. In some ways the formal self-assessment is a reflection of where the business is with its operational performance and a setting of targets and actions for the next period. At the end of that period they will sit down and review if they achieved what they set out to achieve and if not why not. Those meetings are based on the retrospect process and the questions discussed in Chapter 8 on learning after doing.

A continuous cycle of improvement

Building the community of practice

The 'river diagram' stopped short of identifying who that operations manager could turn to for help.

'If I'm at level 3, who can I talk to who is at level 4 or 5?'

This important question needed an answer, so we created a second picture that revealed which businesses had which scores – a way for businesses that wanted to learn to identify who best to learn from.

Putting people in touch with people who can help

We found a simple, yet powerful way to represent these two axes – performance and gap – in a way that revealed which businesses had an appetite for learning, and from whom they could learn.

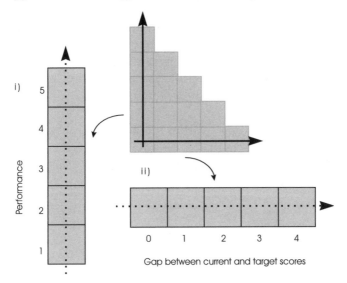

i) illustrates the performance axis

ii) is a measure of the appetite to improve that the business has for this particular issue – the size of the gap between the current score and the target score.

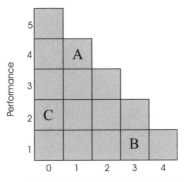

iii) Plotting both axes together leads to a 'set of stairs'.

Business A has a strong performance (4), and an 'improvement gap' of 1 unit – i.e. they aspire to reach level 5. Business B has a low performance at level 1, but an aggressive target to improve by 3 units – they aspire to reach level 4. Finally, Business C has a score of 2, but no improvement target – that particular practice is simply not a priority issue for them.

This mapping of performance against priority makes it easy for business B to identify the businesses from whom they could learn – business A in this case. Once we had populated a series of these 'staircases' with our hundred businesses, we could begin to operate as a dating agency, and encourage meetings, workshops and peer assists that brought together the high performers with the businesses with the strongest desire to learn.

We found that different zones within the diagram indicated where the most powerful interactions lay – between those with successful performance and those with a strong demand for knowledge.

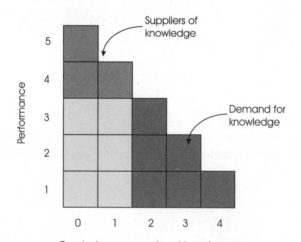

Gap between current and target scores

The steps for putting those who know with those who want to learn

In summary, what could have been a simple league table of performance which drove defensive and competitive behaviours into the company actually became a vehicle for knowledge sharing which acknowledged high-performing businesses, and encouraged others to seek out their help. There were some peer challenges to the relative positions of different businesses and that was healthy. After all the scores are only self-perceptions and led to a dialogue as to what was good practice.

> Think about the practices that you might measure in your organisation, and imagine that you had a 'set of stairs' for each area that mapped both performance and gap. What might it tell you?

'Who is good at customer retention?'

'Who has the strongest desire to improve their use of e-commerce?'

'Who is best in class at quality control?'

'Who could make the best use of our good practice in call centre efficiency?'

'Who else wants to dramatically improve their approach to competitor analysis?

When these important questions can be easily answered by *anyone*, knowledge sharing gets a fresh impetus.

Offers and requests – lessons from the nudist beach!

I can't confess to have any naturist tendencies whatsoever. The idea of taking off all my clothes on a public beach... well, call me a prude, but it's decidedly *un*-natural for me!

Asking for help – an unnatural act?

However, if I absolutely *had to*, I suppose I'd rather go naked on a nudist beach than anywhere else – at least I would be in an environment created for people in a similar state of vulnerability.

One consequence of our macho 'engineering culture' is that *asking for help* is unnatural. Some people feel vulnerable when they admit that they could benefit from the experience of others; consequently, asking for help can feel like a show of weakness.

In designing the operations excellence process, we recognised this aspect of our culture and set out to create the organisational equivalent of a nudist beach for macho operations managers who needed help. Now that *is* frightening imagery – let's move swiftly on!

Here's what we did. As part of the process, after completion of the assessment we added one final stage. Every business was encouraged to make 'three offers and three requests'. An 'offer' in this context is an offer of expertise or help, based on a particular strength, complete with individual contact names and details.

Some examples:

> *'Within Canada Gas we have every employee involved in community activities within the regions we operate. We have an excellent reputation and are happy to share the ways in which we have set up these relationships.'*

> *'Pasadena has extensive experience in the area of managing contract and third party staff, as a result of the plant/business acquisition in 1996. We have a lot of lessons-learned to share regarding contract working, relationship management, and cost control. Note that these lessons-learned encompass both good and not-so-good experiences!'*

> *'Texas City's offer: over the last 2 years have significantly improved safety performance. We offer to share experience of two main initiatives – Advanced Safety Auditing and site wide communication'*

A 'request' is a specific appeal for assistance – for example:

> *'Our Pipeline System spans some 150 kilometres onshore and involves several distinct assets. We generally need to improve shift handover routines and basic communication within our organisation and between sites. We'd welcome some new ideas on good handover/communication techniques. What do you do that's different?'*

> *'We often end up losing more production than originally planned during shutdowns, mainly because of problems on restart, (We deliver shutdown within the planned time-frame but take longer*

than planned to get back to full stable production). Often the problems that caused the delayed return to full production are to do with parts of the plant we didn't touch during the shutdown. We would like to learn from others who have overcome these problems.'

'We request examples of processes used to maintain morale and motivation in a very challenging business environment where the site performance must improve significantly very quickly.'

By institutionalising this exchange of offers and requests into the overall process, we defused the awkwardness of asking for help, and the self-conscious modesty that might prevent businesses feeling that they had anything to contribute. *'Everybody is doing it, so what are* your *three offers and requests?'*

Removing the stigma of asking for help

The list of offers and requests was made available to all staff through a website, working in a similar manner to an online dating agency. As a way to further reinforce the principle, we created and distributed one thousands packs of actual playing cards based on the offers that had been made. Each card featuring a photograph of the individual with a brief headline detailing their expertise – see the examples below.

Another thing we are doing to develop the community is to set up peer assist meetings, or workshops, to discuss areas of common interest. One example of this was a workshop on the subject of reliability at a

*Using informal
approaches to
publicise
where the good
practices lie*

high performing refinery in Castellon, Spain. Representatives from a high-performing chemicals factory and a North Sea production platform, joined Castellon along with staff from different businesses that wanted to improve their reliability. Within 30 minutes participants were in animated conversation, realising they had similar problems and were talking a common language. The conversation did not flag for two days till it was time to return to their own sites. Every one left with ideas of how to improve reliability – even the high performing sites. The event was captured on video and distilled to a CD-ROM-based knowledge asset for wider use.

A community website

In addition to the well-defined process, we commissioned a smart web-based environment to support the exchange of good practices, offers and requests throughout the operations community of 30,000 staff.

*A community
centre*

Through this, we have provided an electronic environment where any of our operations staff can:

- publish news items, upcoming events of interest and success stories into a shared 'newspaper';

- participate in discussion forums on technical subjects;

- view all the offers and requests made to date;

- discover who else was connected to the website at that moment in time and initiate a chat session with them;

- conduct the assessment on-line, generating a customised 'river diagram' for their business in real-time; and

- discover tools to help improve performance in a specific practice, and provide a review of that tool in a similar manner to the book reviews in Amazon.com.

This web-based 'community space' is hosted by a full-time operations professional. He acts as a focal point for this huge community of operators around the world, canvassing them for successes, initiating conversations, chats and discussion threads.

Capturing the knowledge

The knowledge has built along with the communities, which both use and nurture it. We have CD-ROMs that contain the distilled good practices and also contain video clips of people who may help.

Building knowledge and community together

On the community website we have a store of useful tools, documents, good practices etc.

We have identified the knowledge gaps through the assessment and river diagram. These are areas in which the company needs to learn more. Action plans are in hand to address these.

In summary, what have we achieved with operations excellence?

In creating this organisation-wide progress we did not consciously use the holistic model except for an occasional review of what else we might do. We had reached the stage of unconscious competence.

- We introduced a new company-wide process based on the creation of a common language, a standard set of measures and a common assessment.

- We created some new ways to visualise overall performance, linking together good performers with those actively seeking improvement.

- We encouraged the sharing of offers and requests across the company to accelerate improvement and overcome cultural barriers to ask for help.

- We created a community that was committed to help each other improve.

- We underpinned all of the above with enabling technology, and supported this with a new role for one of our operations supervisors.

And we achieved this without mentioning the words 'knowledge management' to anyone!

So that's three areas we have found to embed our KM principles. Soon we will move on to other areas, comfortable that the processes in place are sustainable.

Have a think: 'Where are the knowledge gaps for your organisation – the ones that if plugged would add significant value?' And then figure out how you can use some of the tools and techniques described earlier in this book to embed them in your business processes.

REVIEW OF THE BOOK –
WHAT DID WE SET OUT TO DO?

What was supposed to happen?

We set out to write a book and tell you about knowledge management; to capture and display for you a vivid picture of what we have learned about managing knowledge in BP over the past five years. We have received, and continue to get, lots of requests about how we 'do' knowledge management inside BP. We have read others' perceptions of what BP does, and we wanted to record our own story of what goes on inside BP and how knowledge management is evolving.

We wanted it to be a practical book; you can read it and instantly do something with your knowledge. We perceived it would fill a gap. It would be readily snapped up in airport bookshops and in business school libraries.

We wanted to acknowledge the contribution to collective learning, of the KM team, and of the varied practitioners throughout our organisation.

What actually happened?

The idea was first articulated on a long transatlantic flight. It's amazing how the reduced oxygen at 35,000 feet makes one so much more creative!

We researched how to write a book. We read one about the topic, we searched the Internet for experiences and we spoke to people who had succeeded. We considered the options. Could we publish it ourselves? Do we need an agent? Where are the gaps in the market? Is there a market? We did some research, but we didn't overdo it.

We got clear on what the book would be about; we worked out the principles and the tools to include. Then we sketched out what needed to go into a proposal. We created the market in our mind.

We chose a chapter each, one for which we knew the subject well and started writing. We swapped chapters and amended each other's. It was a real test of how well we, having very different styles of working, could work together.

We had several publishers interested; we selected one we could work with. Our criteria for selection changed. We went for one that believed in the subject we were writing about and one that had fresh ideas.

We had lots of informal reviews. After editing each other's chapters we agreed common approaches before writing the next. We found ourselves looking at books through different lenses. It gave us ideas about which books work and which don't.

We agreed which chapters we would write individually; we worked on those in which we had most interest and most experience. The rest we wrote together.

We put the pages up on the wall, sorted by chapter; in effect we created our own 'War room'. We spotted that the first few chapters set the context and model, and the next set are the tools and techniques. Amazingly we hadn't spotted that distinction before!

As we finished a chapter we sent it to the publisher and requested feedback so that we could build that learning into what we wrote next. They challenged us to include a wider range of stories, beyond BP. We realised we wanted to use stories within our own experience, within BP, but we wanted to find a way to make it relevant to people in smaller organisations. We did that by telling stories and by asking questions to get the reader to reflect. Well did we?

The book came together faster than we expected. The story was easy to tell. We had estimated the time we were prepared to spend on it and estimated the number of words per chapter. We worked best writing with the flow, then editing it afterwards. Collecting the information together then arranging it proved to be clumsy.

We have written a book that describes the fruits of our own experiences in the same way that we might tell a colleague. Knowledge management is a simple idea. The hard bit is in the doing.

What was different between what happened and what was meant to happen?

We delivered ahead of plan, partly because we kept each other honest, and partly because the birth of Hannah was there as a milestone. We thought it would require more in terms of sacrifice of time at home.

We said we would create Internet-style pages. In fact we have created a knowledge asset. It is consistent with our model. In writing this book we have lived and breathed the principles we espouse.

We made explicit the division between the first half about a model and a context for knowledge management and a second half about tools for knowledge management.

We found writing enjoyable rather than a chore, there was something missing when we got to the end.

What have we learned?

We have learned that we can step outside of our area of expertise (neither of us has written a book before) and use the principles of knowledge management to get very quickly up the learning curve.

The exercise has proved to be a good health check on where we are with knowledge management in BP. We found what was truly sustainable within the company. The act of writing it down helped clarify our learning; we have converted tacit to explicit.

'Having read that chapter I finally got it.'

It has made us realise that we have made some progress but there is much more to do.

We learned once again that people are important. The relationship with the publisher is important. We made direct requests of people and were never refused. We asked other authors for advice, we asked for endorsements, for quotes, for review. People were always supportive and constructive.

We learned that our driving force for writing the book was wanting to tell the story our way, not making money, nor building our reputation.

We learned to complement each other's different styles until we could finish each other's sentences!

Incidentally in case you are still curious, BP have made significant progress in gaining the necessary approvals to make the project work in Vietnam, producing gas offshore in the Nam Con Son basin, piping it ashore, processing it, converting it to electricity to supply the major cities of Vietnam to help their industry grow.

And we did get that kitchen finished, and we are proud to invite our dinner guests into the kitchen, sometimes we don't quite move out! But we've never cooked the television presenter's favourite dish, Coquilles St. Jacques with mange tout and fried potato wafers.

Appendix A
Storyboard

In pulling together feedback for a peer assist it is good to let the whole team of visitors work together on the feedback. If it is left to one or two to construct the presentation then often the feedback loses some of its richness. We have found the storyboarding technique useful if involving everybody in creating the story.

Usually we work around a flipchart to focus everyone on the same page.

The first thing to agree on is the purpose of the presentation or feedback. In the case of a peer assist it is usually to highlight what has been done well and some options and insights for improving the final activity or project.

Agree the purpose

Identify the three key messages you want your audience to leave with. By limiting it to only three will demand some discussion of priorities and what will really make the difference. By focussing on the messages you want the audience to leave with ensures you give some thought to how your feedback lands rather than just what you want to tell them. For instance if you say 'Here are two areas where you didn't involve the right people', the message received might be 'they think we should have asked for their opinion earlier'.

Identify the three key messages

Having identified the three key messages divide a flipchart page into eight equal frames. In the first one write 'Intro and Purpose' and in the last one write 'three key messages'.

Take the first key message. What are the important points to get across? Draw a picture and the three or four associated points.

Note the three points to make

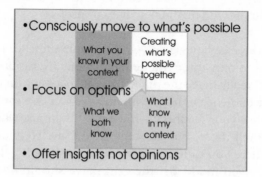

Use between one and three frames to address each message. Once you have finished, look through the flow. What have you missed? Would it be better if you reordered it? If you were receiving this feedback how would it land? Would you walk away with the desired three key messages?

Here's an example of a storyboard for explaining the peer assist process.

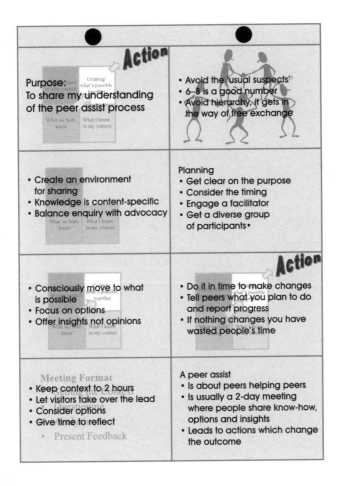

Purpose:
To share my understanding of the peer assist process

- Avoid the 'usual suspects'
- 6–8 is a good number
- Avoid hierarchy, it gets in the way of free exchange

- Create an environment for sharing
- Knowledge is content-specific
- Balance enquiry with advocacy

Planning
- Get clear on the purpose
- Consider the timing
- Engage a facilitator
- Get a diverse group of participants•

- Consciously move to what is possible
- Focus on options
- Offer insights not opinions

- Do it in time to make changes
- Tell peers what you plan to do and report progress
- If nothing changes you have wasted people's time

Meeting Format
- Keep context to 2 hours
- Let visitors take over the lead
- Consider options
- Give time to reflect
- Present Feedback

A peer assist
- Is about peers helping peers
- Is usually a 2-day meeting where people share know-how, options and insights
- Leads to actions which change the outcome

Appendix B

Operations Excellence Practices

1 Use the right people and processes

- Lead and communicate effectively
- Manage asset and organisational effectiveness
- Develop and assure competency
- Raise morale and motivation
- Drive performance improvement
- Share, transfer and embed know-how
- Enhance our reputation with community

2 Cause no harm to people or the environment

- Getting HSE Right
- Manage Greenhouse Gas emissions (GHG)
- Manage water

3 Eliminate unplanned outages

- Manage production losses
- Exploit good reliability processes
- Manage integrity
- Operate equipment reliably

4 Effectively prioritise and execute planned work

- Plan, schedule and execute work
- Prepare and execute turnarounds

5 Optimise production

- Optimise plant performance
- Satisfy customers
- Exploit advanced production technology

6 Minimise cost

- Manage OPEX budget
- Manage contracted (3rd party) services
- Manage process consumable costs
- Manage spare parts and stores
- Manage energy costs and efficiency
- Manage working capital

Resources

One-Page Resources

1

The pages in this section have been designed for you to re-use. Please feel free to photocopy, apply and share them. They are also available electronically as downloads from http://www.learning-to-fly.org

Learning from your Peers

– Somebody has Already Done it

1. *Communicate the purpose.* Peer assists work well when the purpose is clear and you communicate that purpose to participants.

2. *Share your peer assist plans with others.* Consider whether someone else has already solved the problem. They may have similar needs.

3. *Identify a facilitator* for the meeting, who is external to the team. The role of the facilitator is to ensure that by managing the process the meeting participants reach the desired outcome.

4. *Schedule a date* for the peer assist. Ensure it is early enough to do something different with what you have learned. Ask yourself 'If I get a result we do not expect, will I have time to do anything about it?'

5. *Invite potential participants* who have the diversity of skills, competencies and experience needed for the peer assist. Six to eight people is ideal. Avoid 'the Usual Suspects'

6. *Get clear on the desired deliverables* of the peer assist (usually options and insights), and then plan the time to achieve that.

7. *Allow time to socialise* in order to develop a team.

8. *Allow a day and a half for the peer assist.* Schedule time to Tell, Ask, Analyse and Feedback.

9. *Create the right environment.* Spend some time creating the right environment for sharing. Plan the event to allow a balance between telling and listening.

10. *Listen for understanding* and how you might improve your activity.

11. *Consider who else might benefit from this knowledge.*

12. *Commit to actions* and keep the peer assist team updated.

Learning Whilst Doing – Time to Reflect

1. *Hold the AAR immediately.* AAR's are carried out immediately whilst all of the participants are still available, and their memories are fresh. Learning can then be applied right away, even on the next day.

2. *Create the right climate.* The ideal climate for an AAR to be successful is one of openness and commitment to learning. Everyone should participate in an atmosphere free from the concept of seniority or rank. AARs are learning events rather than critiques. They certainly should not be treated as personal performance evaluation.

3. *Appoint a facilitator.* The facilitator of an AAR is not there to 'have' answers, but to help the team to 'learn' answers. People must be drawn out, both for their own learning and the group's learning.

4. *Ask 'what was supposed to happen?'* The facilitator should start by dividing the event into discrete activities, each of which had (or should have had) an identifiable objective and plan of action. The discussion begins with the first activity: 'What was supposed to happen?'

5. *Ask 'what actually happened?'* This means the team must understand and agree facts about what happened. Remember, though, that the aim is to identify a problem not a culprit.

6. *Now compare the plan with reality.* The real learning begins as the team of teams compares the plan to what actually happened in reality and determines 'Why were there differences?' and 'What did we learn?' Identify and discuss successes and shortfalls. Put in place action plans to sustain the successes and to improve upon the shortfalls.

7. *Record the key points.* Recording the key elements of an AAR clarifies what happened and compares it to what was supposed to happen. It facilitates sharing of learning experiences within the team and provides the basis for a broader learning programme in the organisation.

Learning After Doing – When it's All Over

1. *Call the meeting.* Hold a face-to-face meeting as soon as you can after the project ends, within weeks rather than months.

2. *Invite the right people.* The project leader needs to attend, as do key members of the project team. If a similar project is underway, then there is great value in the new project team attending.

3. *Appoint a facilitator.* Identify a facilitator who was not closely involved in the project.

4. *Revisit the objectives and deliverables of the project.* Ask 'what did we set out to do?' and 'what did we achieve?'

5. *Ask 'what went well?'* Ask 'what were the successful steps towards achieving your objective?' and 'what went really well in the project?' Ask a 'why?' question several times. This will get you to the root of the reason.

6. *Find out why these aspects went well, and express the learning as advice for the future.* Acknowledge feelings and press for the facts. Ask 'what repeatable, successful processes did we use?' and 'how could we ensure future projects go just as well, or even better?'.

7. *Ask 'what could have gone better?'* Ask 'what were the aspects that stopped you delivering even more?' Identify the stumbling blocks and pitfalls, so they can be avoided in future by asking 'what would your advice be to future project teams, based on your experiences here?'

8. *Record the meeting.* Use quotes to express the depth of feeling. Express the recommendations as clearly, measurably and unambiguously as possible. Ensure that you circulate the write-up around the participants for comment before sharing more widely.

Finding the Right People – If Only I Knew Who

1. *Maintain a clear and distinctive vision.* Be clear about what you are trying to achieve and avoid compromise. Beware of becoming 'all things to all men' – particularly those in the HR and IT departments!

2. *Strive for personal ownership and maintenance.* Create a process whereby only the individuals concerned can create and update their entries. This will drive a far deeper sense of ownership across the population.

3. *Strike a balance between informal and formal content.* Encourage people to share non-work information about themselves in addition to valuable business information.

4. *Support the photographs wherever possible.* Nothing is more powerful and personal than a photograph. It speaks volumes about the person, raises the interest levels of others and generates personal ownership of the content.

5. *Ensure that your product design is flexible and inclusive.* Recognise that different people relate to templates and structure in different ways. Use focus groups to test opinion.

6. *Start with a customer-facing pilot.* Critical mass is all important, so start with a group of people who have a natural need to be visible to internal customers.

7. *Deliver through local enthusiasts.* Centrally-driven push isn't always the best way to engage the workforce. Tap into local enthusiasts if possible.

8. *Use success stories as a marketing tool.* Reinforce the usefulness of the knowledge directory at every opportunity. Publicise any examples or successes widely.

9. *Encourage use, but lead by example rather than edict.* Avoid mandating the population and use of the knowledge directory. People will provide better quality content if they feel that they are volunteering the information

10. *Embed into people processes.* Look for process 'hooks' that could initiate and sustain the use of your knowledge directory (e.g. recruitment or induction).

Learning to Fly © Chris Collison and Geoff Parcell, 2001

Networking and Communities of Practice

1. *Quick wins come from sharing what we know* across the organisation.

2. *Provide a website and a discussion forum.* This is used for sharing key documents, standards, a common model, procedures and in particular the contact details of members.

3. Determine whether the community is about developing the capability of the individual (*enabling network*), or collectively accountable for delivering a business objective (*delivery network*).

4. *Establish a clear, simple governing document.* Typically an enabling network has a terms of reference, and a delivery network has a set of objectives or performance contract agreed with a sponsor.

5. *Identify and refresh membership,* as people leave and join according to their changing needs. Welcome new members with a personal e-mail or phone call.

6. *Meet face-to-face* and allow for socialisation. Formal networks should aim to meet face-to-face at least once a year to establish and maintain relationships. Avoid cramming the agenda and allow plenty of time for socialising at these gatherings.

7. *Sustain the network by identifying a coordinator* whose role it is to help others share and stimulate collaboration.

8. *Delivery networks thrive on support from senior management.* Identify a business sponsor to agree objectives and a functional mentor to provide assurance coaching and resources.

9. *Consider the community as guardians of the company's knowledge.* Expect them to keep the knowledge valid, accessible and refreshed.

Leveraging What We've Learned – Capturing Knowledge

1. *Identify a customer for this knowledge.* Have a clear customer – current or future – in mind when considering the creation of a knowledge asset.

2. *Get clear what your knowledge asset is really about.* What is the scope of your knowledge asset? A knowledge asset needs to cover a specific area of business activity.

3. *Identify a community of practice relating to this subject.* The community will be the source of the knowledge in the first place the users of the knowledge in future, and the people who validate the knowledge in the knowledge asset.

4. *Collate any existing material upon which you can base your knowledge asset and look for general guidelines.* Provide some context so that people can understand the purpose and relevance of the knowledge asset. Are there general guidelines that you can distil out of this material?

5. *Build a checklist illustrated with examples and stories.* The checklist should tell the user of the knowledge asset:
    'What are the questions I need to ask myself?'
    'What are the steps that I need to take?'
    Illustrate it with examples, stories, pictures, models, quotes, video and audio clips if possible.

6. *Include links to people.* Create a hyperlink to the persons personal home page or e-mail address wherever you mention them in the text. Include a list of all the people with any relationship with the content.

7. *Validate the guidelines.* Circulate the guidelines around the community again, and ask 'Do the guidelines accurately reflect your knowledge and experience?' 'Do you have anything to add?'

8. *Publish the knowledge asset.* Store the knowledge in a space where it can be accessed by its community. Often this will mean the company intranet.

9. *Initiate a feedback and ownership process.* Encourage feedback from users, so that they pick up and eliminate any invalid recommendations. Instil a sense of obligation that 'if you use it, then you should add to it'.

Learning to Fly © Chris Collison and Geoff Parcell, 2001

Resources

Inspirational reading, people and technologies

In writing this chapter, we wanted to avoid providing an all-inclusive library of knowledge management materials – the Internet has several of these. We have identified here the materials that you would find on our desks today if you came into our office! We have included books and papers that we have really read and applied, the people who have inspired us, and the technologies which have made a difference.

1. Setting the Context

   • Your company's annual report!

2. What is Knowledge Management?

   • *The Knowledge-Creating Company: How Japanese Companies Create the Dynamics of Innovation*, Ikujiro Nonaka, Hirotaka Takeuchi, Hiro Takeuchi.

   • *Working Knowledge*, Thomas Davenport, Laurence Prusak.

   • Prokesch, Steven E. (1997) 'Unleashing the Power of Learning: An interview with British Petroleum's John Browne' *HBR* September–October.

   • Knowledge Transformations International (http://www.ktransform.com). A consultancy formed by several former members of BP's knowledge management team, specialising in coaching, facilitation, training and support.

3. The Holistic Model – it's More than the Sum of the Parts

- *Information Space: A framework for Learning in Organizations, Institutions and Culture*, Max H. Boisot.

4. Getting the Environment Right

- Argyris, Chris (1991) 'Teaching Smart People How to Learn' *Harvard Business Review*, May–June, pp. 99–109.

- *Simplicity: The New Competitive Advantage in a World of More, Better, Faster*, Bill Jensen.

- *The Fifth Discipline Fieldbook: Strategies and Tools for Building a Learning Organization*, Peter Senge.

5. Getting Started – Just Do It

- No resources needed – just you, and this book!

6. Learning from your Peers –Somebody has Already Done it

- One page summary on 'Peer Assists' (see p. 206).

7. Learning Whilst Doing – Time to Reflect

- Center for Army Lessons Learned – Leader's guide to After Action Reviews, http://call.army.mil/call/trngqtr/tq2%2D98/guide.htm.

- One page summary on 'Reviewing what you have done' (see p. 207).

8. Learning After Doing – When it's All Over

- One page summary on 'Learning After Doing – When it's All Over' (see p. 208).

9. Finding the Right People – If Only I Knew Who

- SigmaConnect knowledge directory used in BP: http://www.sigmaconnect.com.

- One page summary on 'Finding the Right People – If Only I Knew Who' (see p. 209).

10. Networking and Communities of Practice

   - Community Intelligence Labs – research network on Communities of Practice: http://www.co-i-l.com/coil/.

   - One page summary on 'Networking and Communities of Practice' (see p. 210).

   - The community of practice for readers of 'Learning to Fly': http://www.learning-to-fly.org.

11. Leveraging What We've Learned – Capturing Knowledge

   - Knowledge Transformations International (http://www.ktransform.com). A consultancy formed by several former members of BP's knowledge management team, specialising in coaching, facilitation, training and support.

   - Henderson, J. C. and Sussman, S. W. (1997) *Creating and Exploiting Knowledge for Fast-Cycle Organizational Response*, The Center for Army Lessons Learned, Boston University Working Paper No 96–39.

   - One page summary on 'Leveraging What We've Learned – Capturing Knowledge' (see p. 211).

12. Embedding it in the Organisation – Preparing to Let Go

   - *The Goal: A process of ongoing improvement* Eliyahu M. Goldratt, Jeff Cox.

13. Review of the Book – What Did We Set Out to Do?

   - Let us know what you learned. Contact the authors by visiting: http://www.learning-to-fly.org

INDEX